Holy Lc

When a person's child deception, they are at risk for creating a life that mirrors the same. This foundation sets the stage for heartache, broken relationships, dysfunctional psychological patterns and more.

Jill E. Smith invites you to share her journey that began in childhood and impacted her well into adulthood. You might even find yourself identifying with some if not most of this shared testimony, because everyone has a story. We all have secrets.

She will share with you the peace she has found and how her life changed course when she discovered her path to Jesus. As she so poignantly states, all of the dramas and sorrows in one's life can create obstacles to inner peace and joy. Most of all, these obstacles prevent us from loving well. Learning how to love well became like a search for the holy grail for the author. It was in this seeking that Jill Smith found healing from her past traumas and sorrows.

The lovely poems, family photos, and images from her garden and front yard that she incorporates into this memoir, will help you to resonate with the message that sorrow can also be a path that can take you to peace and healing.

Jill Smith opens the window of her heart and takes us on her childhood journey of pain and heartbreak. Her redemptive testimony resulting in love and forgiveness to the one who caused her so much pain, powerfully illustrates the essence of being authentic and selfless. Like Jill, may we all allow God to make beauty out of ashes, joy out of mourning and a garment of praise from a spirit of despair.

Dawn Pickett
Homeschool high school history teacher
Fellowship of Christian Athletes-USA

I highly recommend this personal testimonial story about the power of God's holy love. Nothing else can transform the heartache of shame but the grace of Jesus.

Tammy Thompson
Co-host of Love and Encouragement to Live By

This is a living testimony of the power of God's grace in the face of everything this world makes itself out to be. I appreciate how Jill has opened up her heart and soul for all to see. On a day when Jill was at a festival selling things that make people look and feel pretty on the outside, she was hurting deeply and had no idea that later that day God had plans to heal as only He can. I absolutely love how Jill has described her walk to her praying neighbor's house on that special day that God had known about before the foundations of world. As she stated "I was heading to the cross---unbeknownst to me, but well known to the enemy." Jill's story is a sobering reminder that for some the journey to the cross is long and hard, but for all who make it, it is well worth it!

Pastor Quintin Merson
CrossLife Bible Church
Westminster, MD

If you live in Mayberry-where everything goes pretty much as planned and life always seems perfect-then this book is probably not for you. Most of us have high expectations for our lives but find ourselves in a broken world often due to poor choices. This passionate book, unflinching in its honesty and vulnerability, reveals the transformation that happens when God is invited into the journey. Jill's story, is a remarkable and reliable companion for those who are hurting, yet hopeful!

Rev. Mark Norman
Pastor Emeritus
Grace Community Church
Fulton, Maryland

Beautifully written journey about healing and coming to wholeness. Jill Smith takes us on a journey of questioning and self-discovery as she explores childhood events that shaped her personality. A childhood fraught with deception left deep wounds that only God could heal. Magic begins as Jill discovers her personal relationship with God. Through this love and comfort, the strength comes to her, to move through these wounds with understanding and forgiveness. Jill inspires the reader, through her journey, to reflect on their own life, and shows us how we can deepen our relationships and heal our pasts.

Sharon Hyde
National Marketing Director
The JuicePlus Company

HOLY LOVE

A Memoir of Sorrow to Glory

Jill E. Smith

WESTBOW
PRESS®
A DIVISION OF THOMAS NELSON
& ZONDERVAN

WestBow Press books may be ordered through booksellers or by contacting:

WestBow Press
A Division of Thomas Nelson & Zondervan
1663 Liberty Drive
Bloomington, IN 47403
www.westbowpress.com
844-714-3454

Because of the dynamic nature of the Internet, any web addresses or links contained in this book may have changed since publication and may no longer be valid. The views expressed in this work are solely those of the author and do not necessarily reflect the views of the publisher, and the publisher hereby disclaims any responsibility for them.

Photography captured and copyrighted by Passionate Portraits
PassionatePortraitsWeb.com

Scripture quotations marked (NLT) are taken from the Holy Bible, New Living Translation, copyright ©1996, 2004, 2015 by Tyndale House Foundation. Used by permission of Tyndale House Publishers, Carol Stream, Illinois 60188. All rights reserved.

Scripture quotations marked (NIV) are taken from the Holy Bible, New International Version®, NIV®. Copyright © 1973, 1978, 1984, 2011 by Biblica, Inc.® Used by permission of Zondervan. All rights reserved worldwide. www.zondervan.com The "NIV" and "New International Version" are trademarks registered in the United States Patent and Trademark Office by Biblica, Inc.®

Scripture marked (KJV) taken from the King James Version of the Bible.

ISBN: 978-1-6642-3411-6 (sc)
ISBN: 978-1-6642-3410-9 (hc)
ISBN: 978-1-6642-3412-3 (e)

Library of Congress Control Number: 2021909617

Print information available on the last page.

WestBow Press rev. date: 11/15/2021

CONTENTS

ACKNOWLEDGEMENTS

This book would never have come to fruition if not for my husband Larry. His support and patience with my unrelenting focus on the writing of my memoir was unwavering. Larry is the quiet warrior in my life who has my back in all of my endeavors. He's brought the joy of music and dancing into my life. His love language manifesting in his Sunday breakfasts brought a savory healing to both me and my daughters as we picked up the remnants of our lives and started over with him in our new home in Catonsville, Maryland. He was once asked, if our marriage were an orchestra, what instruments would we be. He said he would be the bass and I would be the trumpet. The bass maintains the foundational home base where all the instruments can meld their melody to. As his trumpet, I am often multi-tasking in activities and ideas. Larry is my home base who reliably stays steady and patient. He has been a stellar stepfather to my two daughters. He has helped in the healing of their hearts as well. Larry has often said "The best gift a father can give his children is to love their mother".

He is my home and my heart and the love of my life.

I also want to acknowledge my neighbors and dear friends Barbara and Greg Hart. Their prayers and love for me saw me through the most challenging time in my life. They invited me to place my burdens at the foot of Jesus's Cross, and for that I will be forever grateful.

And finally, I want to thank Tammy Thompson (Portrait Passions), my editor and photographer and friend. Her committed work in helping me to organize and edit my memoir took months of dedication. I could not have taken this book to publication without her skill and expertise, as well as her prayerful guidance and reassurance.

DEDICATION TO
MY DAUGHTERS

A gentle spirit is she…my first.
Concealed awareness of the heart of another.
Searching for her rainbows.
Resisting relinquishing her innocence.
Her flushing face would expose her hurt.
And her joy would burst forth in love!
Her gentle spirit preserved within the strength of her character.
True grit is what I'd call her from time to time.
Her name rolled off my tongue like a musical note.
And she blossoms with such loveliness.
Motherhood has served her well.

Exuberance…right there…my second.
Her voice shouting with such delight and joy
that even the seagulls take note.
The waves collide with the shore line.
Their saltiness smacks against the sand.
I don't have to watch her because her
voice cascades above the waves.
And her laughter.
She is joy personified!
Her voice commands the waves to meld to the will of her laughter.
And her squeals outshine the seagulls with delight.
I do not have to search for her in the
frothy wetness or the salty mist.
My heart smiles as I listen for her with the vigilance of a mother.

PREFACE

You must not commit adultery.
Exodus 20:14 (NLT)

*Teach me your ways, O Lord, that I may live according
to your truth! Grant me purity of heart,
so that I may honor you. With all my heart I will
praise you, O Lord my God. I will give glory to your
name forever, for your love for me is great.
You have rescued me from the depths of death.*
Psalm 86: 11-13 (NLT)

This is a book authored by me in partnership with the Holy
Spirit. I've concluded that my story as the daughter of an
adulterous mother is the vehicle that Jesus has used to share His own
message. I am co-author of *Holy Love: A Memoir of Sorrow to Glory*.

Over time I've discovered that the Holy Spirit works through
us, and so I've learned how to get out of my own way when Jesus
compels me to take pen in hand. Some are inspired writings, which
I like to call "my musings with the Lord." Some passages are in the
first person as if I am speaking or praying directly to Him. Then
others are my recorded events that led to my transformation from a
wandering Jew to a born-again Christian. I find myself drawn to the
term 'wandering Jew' because of my distant ancestors who wandered
through the desert for forty years so that they could ultimately enter
the Promised Land that God had chosen for them.

As I neared the end of this manuscript, I found myself being
delivered from the shame and sorrow that had clung to me all

of my life. Choosing to partner with the Holy Spirit, this book became a healing journey. I did not set out in search of healing. It evolved delightfully in the course of the writing. The trajectory of the manuscript will reveal to you this transition from suffering to freedom and joy. As the shame and sorrows slowly and subtly evaporated, the space that opened up left room for my capacity to learn how to love with all my heart. In that process, God blessed me with insights into Holy Love. Like the sun peeking through the space between clouds, God would reveal to me in milli-moments visions of His design for us for Holy Love. This journey from the scorched earth of my former life as a Jew who didn't know Jesus into the lush valley of His glorious garden is where I discovered His Holy Love.

I have marveled at the juxtaposition from where I embarked and where I finally ended up. Loving well is the place I felt most crippled, and yet God used that brokenness along with my sin to illuminate Himself on paper. I find it a mystery that God would give me the challenge to illuminate for you His Holy Love.

My prayer for those reading this is to experience a quickening desire and an inspiration to know Yeshua/Jesus better. I hope the glimpses into Holy Love on these pages will call you to Him and nudge you to seek Him as I did. Yeshua/Jesus is waiting for your heart to open to His, because that is where our capacity to love our most cherished will deepen and flourish.

But from there you will search again for the Lord your God. And if you search for him with all your heart and soul you will find him.
Deuteronomy 4:29 (NLT)

PROLOGUE

And since we are his children, we are his heirs.
In fact, together with Christ we are heirs of God's glory. But if we
are to share his glory, we must also share his suffering. Yet what we
suffer now is nothing compared to the glory he will reveal to us later.
Romans 8:17-18 (NLT)

It was Tuesday, September 15, 2009. I gazed out my office window toward the grounds of the psychiatric hospital a few miles away. It dominated the hill just beyond my view. I wondered if I should simply drive in that direction when my day was over, voluntarily check myself in, and surrender myself to the world.

My fourteen-year-old daughter had left me. I'd lost her. This was the exuberant smiling little girl who at nine years old would still hold my hand in the parking lot. She was the one who still loved to ride on the grocery cart as we shopped together. Even at fourteen she'd beg to lick the chocolate batter off of the baking spatula. She was my baking 'taste-tester'.

My daughter had decided to move in with her father and stepmother. My closest friends promised me it could never happen. "The maternal bond is too strong," they said. But at that moment, on that day, that basic truth shattered, and nothing made sense.

I felt I had lost my mind, as if the foundation I stood on, the rock I had thought was sacred, had tumbled into the depths of oblivion. Overwhelmed by the weight of my broken heart and the sense of the failure of my life, I felt that her leaving was my fault.

The skyline was vast on this clear and sunny morning as I handed over my shattered dreams to the Lord. I envisioned myself holding my love-worn teddy bear. It represented my children and my motherhood journey thus far.

I took my limp doll and held it up toward Him. Whimpering like a seven-year-old little girl I pleaded with Him, "Please forgive me, Father, I broke it. I'm sorry. Please, Father, fix it. Forgive me. I broke it."

Then He spoke into my dark vast ocean of despair and His breath surrounded me with these words, "You were never here to mother your daughters in the flesh. You are here to love them with holiness like Mary loved Jesus."

At that moment, the myriad of broken promises and shattered dreams of my childhood merged into those of my motherhood experience. My silent sorrow, which had become so gripping, began to dissolve in an instant. It felt like a vise around my heart had suddenly released. I knew that it was only Jesus who could crack the seal of that painful chamber and open that heavy door. It was only His light that could shine into my darkness and offer me hope.

Suddenly it was all so clear and pristinely simple. Instantaneously, the mountain of pain bearing down upon me lifted. Like a puff of wind on a pile of ashes, it vanished. Only God has the power to do that!

I didn't know at that moment in September 2009 that His loving words would become the inspiration for my life and this book. The conviction to write this book took another six years to come to fruition, and in obedience, I am duty-bound to share my story with as much transparency as possible.

SHOW ME LORD

Show me Lord,
Show me what You want me to see.
Remove any blinders from my eyes
and reveal Your gifts to me.
Lord, help me paint Your pasture into words.
Guide my hand to brush the strokes of
Your artistry into words on paper.
Fleeting moments of Your light sparkle between
two people and the vast landscape
of Your love is revealed.
I've felt it...I know it's You...and I want to share it!
I want to help the world see it too, so it will know what to look for.
In this broken world where we tend to exist in the underbelly
of life's shadow, we forget to revel in the sweetness of our most
cherished relationships and moments. We don't even know it's
there when it's right in front of us. We gaze past it or beyond it.
It's right in front of us but we don't know how to focus on it.
It's You, sweet Jesus, who exists in that light;
in that space between two people.
You are the bridge that bonds the gap between
people. Your Holy Love is the glue;
the sap that provides the eternal nourishment that we hunger for.

CHAPTER 1

The Floodgates Broke

*Jesus replied, "I assure you, no one can enter the
Kingdom of God without being born of water and the Spirit.
Humans can reproduce only human life, but the Holy Spirit
gives birth to spiritual life. So don't be surprised when I say,
'You must be born again'. The wind blows wherever it wants.
Just as you can hear the wind but can't tell where it comes
from or where it is going, so you can't explain how
people are born of the Spirit."*
John 3:5-8 (NLT)

It had been a few weeks since that stunning moment in my office.
It had also been a few weeks since I "came to Christ" in my next-door neighbor's living room. My neighbors Barbara and Greg had discipled me during the tumultuous summer of 2009, which had culminated in my daughter choosing to move away. They were giddy with joy over my accepting Christ as my Savior. However, from my perspective my life was still in shambles. My daughter was gone and everything paled in comparison to that one painful reality. Coming to Jesus felt merely intellectual for me in the days following that scene in their living room. I'll elaborate on this event later.

As I replayed the events of that day in my neighbor's home in my mind, I stepped into the shower for my morning ritual to ease my stiff muscles and let the sorrow cascade down the drain. The hot water loosened my rigid muscles, which were still working overtime in their practiced pattern of protecting my mind and body. Tight muscles were the hallmark of my life up to this point. The tautness was my norm. I knew nothing else beyond the brief hours after a massage when it felt like my sinews would breathe deeply for a bit. It was like a fish that doesn't know it's in water until it isn't; predictably my muscles would return to their armored state by each day's end. Tight muscles were my signature as far back as I could remember and I didn't know anything else.

On this morning, it was not only the water slapping my shoulders that I could hear. God also spoke to me. In the midst of the heat and the steam and my sadness, He broke through my shell of sorrow and spoke into my heart with such love that all I could do was burst into sobs. He made me see, with such precision, the magnitude of my rejection of His love. It was as if the soothing hot water became icy pellets as the sudden recognition of my own pride pierced my heart.

I was acutely aware of His presence and my deep regret and contrition. I could only speak the words "I'm so sorry." Repeatedly I cried out amongst the flood of regret, "I am so sorry!" My sobs echoed off the porcelain tiles as His conviction and His love washed over me.

I could see and feel the magnitude of my pride as if it was a separate entity or a living organism. So massive in its weight and substance that all I could do was gaze upon it with repentance. It was as if, for the first time in my fifty-five years on this earth, my pride had left my body and stood in all its monolithic presence before me. My pride surrounded me and nearly enveloped me, but it was no longer inside of me. Its oppressive presence was in stark contrast to the love of Jesus, who simply gazed down at me with acceptance and mercy.

Jesus knew my heart. He understood my need to control all the aspects of my life. He had watched me glean a sense of identity from my own accomplishments. My sense of being 'good enough of a person' was defined by my own perspective of the world. Everything I did, and every decision I made was about protecting my own wounds that I'd garnered in my nearly six decades on this earth. How could I feel so utterly exposed and vulnerable at that moment in the shower, yet have no fear or shame. No painful guilt.

Jesus was love. He was so profoundly accepting and forgiving that in his presence, all I could do was weep and drop to my knees and ask for forgiveness and receive the new life only He could offer me. The hot water rained down upon me as my pride began its erosive dismantling down the drain. In many ways, the story of my new life began that morning in the shower.

The intimacy of my connection to Jesus is like a precious diamond. Looking back at that pivotal moment in my life, I've come to understand that any one person's relationship to Christ is profound and unique. Therein lies the holiness of the romance. The start of this relationship is so intimate and the ensuing journey is equally personal in its process.

Out of my service and love of Jesus, a newfound willingness to learn how to relinquish my pride and its hold on my life was born. This set the stage for Jesus to reveal to me the path of discovery of how to love with all my heart. In the end, as in Jesus, it is all about love.

A fifty-five-year journey led me to this life-altering moment. It did not come with ease. It came with angst and sorrow that permeated every breath I had taken up to that point. I invite you to follow me on this journey I took from shame and sorrow to love.

Remember that the Lord rescued you from the iron-smelting furnace of Egypt in order to make you his very own people and his special possession, which is what you are today.
Deuteronomy 4:20 (NLT)

CHAPTER 2

Born into Deceit

*The adulteress waits for the twilight, Saying, "No one will
see me then." She hides her face so no one will know her.*
Job 24:15 (NLT)

Mine is a story of brokenness and deliverance. It illuminates a
journey from sorrow to glory. It's a story of God's unending
and patient pursuit of me and His longing for my return. Ultimately,
it was a quest whose sole purpose was to return to and glorify Him,
and in the end, discover Holy Love.

> *I will give them hearts that recognize me as the Lord.
> They will be my people, and I will be their God,
> for they will return to me wholeheartedly.*
> **Jeremiah 24:7 (NLT)**

Someone asked me what I meant by the words *return to Him*.
We are His creation, and it is a personal and intentional relationship
He desires with us. Hence, my life is an illustration of the return to
my first love. Thus, the psalmist describes the intimacy which God
had with him:

> *For you created my inmost being; you knit me together in
> my mother's womb. I praise you because I am fearfully and
> wonderfully made; your works are wonderful, I know that full*

well. My frame was not hidden from you when I was made in the secret place, when I was woven together in the depths of the earth. Your eyes saw my unformed body; all the days ordained for me were written in your book before one of them came to be.
Psalm 139: 13-16 (NIV)

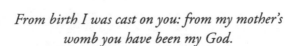

From birth I was cast on you: from my mother's womb you have been my God.
Psalm 22:10 (NIV)

May 13, 1954, is the moment of my biological birth. Mine was an unplanned pregnancy to parents who loved me dearly. It was unplanned because my mother was still adjusting to motherhood with a nine-month-old.

Motherhood did not come with ease for my mother. It could not have been an easy path for her. I know this because my mother was an adulteress. How could a woman not struggle when she is living two separate lives?

I was the middle child of a suburban Jewish family. My sister was eighteen months older than me, and my brother was six years younger. My sister was my best friend and primary playmate, and I loved my little brother unconditionally. I had a devoted father and a beautiful mother. We had two dogs, and sometimes three. We lived on a typical suburban tree-lined street in a brick rancher. On the surface, we went through the motions of a family well. There were family drives, which were a popular outing at the time. There were barbecues and family trips to the beach. We were a typical Jewish family, but within our walls lurked hidden secrets and manipulations; deception and adultery.

My life was a fraudulent one. When family life is built around the deception of adultery, it becomes hollow. I was a Jewish girl wandering through life seeking something I didn't consciously know. I carried a gnawing discomfort and edginess that belied the seemingly sweet, obedient little girl of an adulterous mother.

Sorrow was my shadow. It became like a blanket to me, surrounding me with comforting predictability like night follows day.

My mother was a Brooklyn, New York girl who was the youngest of nine children. She was surrounded by multiple parenting figures, as one would expect. She grew to be a strikingly beautiful woman. I used to describe her as Marilyn Monroe with black hair. Her dark brown eyes that sparkled with an easy smile were mesmerizing to men, and her body was blessed with the voluptuousness that was most valued by the culture at that time. She was a sweet woman. My mom loved to dance and sing with her lovely voice and always promised someday to take singing lessons. She also loved to draw and paint, with the promise of one day taking professional art classes.

Sadly, she never did any of those things. She didn't excel in her God-given talents but rather excelled at reveling in her beauty. Men adored her, as did my father. I'd marvel at the heads that turned in her direction as she walked into a roomful of people.

She was charming with a good sense of humor. I loved it when she'd teach me how to dance to Motown music. I loved gazing down into the living room and watching her dance with my father at the parties they liked to have in our home. Seeing them enjoying life together in those moments filled me with joy and pride.

I recall her reading to my sister and me at night in our bedroom. She had that promise of a nightly ritual, and I even remember her teaching us to pray at bedtime: "Now I lay me down to sleep, I pray the Lord my soul to keep. And if I should die before I wake, I pray to God my soul to take."

My siblings and I were very obedient children, so in many respects, we made her job as a mother easy. My mom was not a harsh disciplinarian nor overly strict with us as children.

She was fun-loving, and my friends always enjoyed coming to my home to visit. What was there to hate? The challenge for the child of such a mother is that it was impossible to hate her. I loved my mother and remained deeply devoted to her throughout my childhood and through the entirety of my adulthood.

My devotion was in part due to the role reversal required of me and my sister. The sense of obligation to protect and support my mother was seared into me like a tattoo. It was a cornerstone of my own identity as I matured. Even after her death in the hospital, I sat vigil, protecting her body until the funeral home arrived to take her away. The hospital staff wanted to bring her body down to the morgue but I wouldn't allow it. I knew she'd hate being alone like that. It was as if the role reversal she had demanded was hard-wired into my psyche.

It may have been easier if she was unloving, hateful, or overly strict and withholding. But she was none of these things. My mother's failings were always clandestine. She hid them from my father and the wives of her numerous lovers. A need for attention from men was an addiction for her. This addiction was so prevailing that she would come to use her daughters as her confidantes so that she could manage her secret life.

Within the walls of my home, my mother shattered the sanctity of both family and marriage. She betrayed the blessings of motherhood and enlisted my sister and me as accomplices to a lifestyle that became like oxygen to her. Her secret life was her sustenance; her children and husband were not.

I think about how attached I was to my family growing up. Looking back, it seems the more elusive and emotionally impoverished my family was, the tighter I held on. The less my mother valued its preciousness, the more I tightened my grip on it, until family itself became an idol to me. My parents referred to me as the family girl. I used to refer to myself as the mortar that held the family together. That became my identity. It gave me a sense of importance in an environment that didn't offer me the value in the integrity and sanctity of family that I hungered for. The sweetness of cherishing each other was absent.

The anguish I would experience in the defiling of my family became the compass of my life. It permeated it. In order to find peace in the sorrow that vibrated just below the surface of my mind, I began a mental process that focused solely on my holding the family together. I began the systematic process of relinquishing my sense of self and my own identity in an effort to keep the family intact.

I celebrated family gatherings with enthusiasm. Having learned to never ask for anything, I deferred to whatever my mother wanted and was obedient to the nth degree. I denied my own urges and impulses until I became so self-controlled and self-reflective that by the time I entered my adolescence, I easily gave up the typical teenage outings and socializing that were the cultural hallmarks of those years.

Beginning at the age of four, I knew something was missing. I knew my life was a lie. Not like a mature adult who knows how to discern truth from lies. Rather, I knew it in an obtuse, gnawing, and unformed way in my gut. I was a child who could only sense and intuit but not yet understand with the wisdom that comes from life experience. My life was that of an idyllic fantasy of family, and I was a little girl with childlike intellect, unable to reconcile this sham.

When I was four, my parents separated for the first time. I recall my mother crying and waking my sister and me out of deep sleep. It was dawn on a Sunday morning as she bundled us up into the back seat of our family car. Out of the second-floor window my father was leaning and shouting at her while she cried shouting back. That morning my idyllic life shattered with the rising of the sun.

We spent the next days or weeks at my cousin's house, while my parents, my grandparents, and extended family worked it out. They worked it out. We returned home to our make-believe life. From that moment on, I never trusted my home life as reality. I began the development of what I would refer to as my antenna. I was an obedient and vigilant child, always waiting for a sign of the collapse of my world as I knew it.

On the surface, all appeared well with the lovely wife and her handsome husband and their two beautiful little girls and adorable son. There was the house with a family dog and a backyard swing set. We did surface well. We continued to take family vacations and had family barbecues, birthday parties, and holiday celebrations. I excelled in school and piano lessons. But a beautiful house that was permeated by adultery and lies was still a house built on sand.

Tainted and spoiled by deception like a scorched pot of soup, my family life left me longing for the love and honor that it was designed for. I pondered if God planted this awareness within me so that I would hunger for something I couldn't define. At four years old, the longing for love and sweetness is an urge without clear intellectual concepts. It's a hunger that permeates everything throughout the day and wee hours of the night. It's like oxygen. Your life depends upon it. And while at such a young age, I couldn't have verbalized that it was missing, God knew, and He beckoned me.

It's not that my parents didn't love me. I actually felt deeply loved by my father. I adored him, and I knew he adored me. This deep-rooted connection felt very different from the one with my mother.

I knew she loved me, but it felt more cerebral. Even now, thirty-four years after his death, I can still feel my father's love, which feels very different from my mother's. There was a visceral, palpable connection between my father and me, which simply showed up missing between me and my mother.

The paradox was that despite her centralness to my life, our connection felt shallow. Her self-absorption thwarted the development of a substantive, deep, and healthy well-rooted love connection. The shallowness of my mother's love became the template of my own experience of love. It shaped the way I would both love and receive love for the next several decades of my life.

◆◆◆◆◆

The name of the Lord is a fortified tower; the righteous run to it and are safe.
Proverbs 18:10 (NIV)

It was the 1950s and one of my favorite spots as a child was my sister's bed, which was against the bedroom window. From that window, I could see our backyard and beyond. Past the yard, I could see the Baltimore WBAL television tower. It was actually about five miles away, but in 1959, it was the tallest television tower in my town. The top of the tower was shaped like a steel-framed box. There were four separate spires that stood tall on each of its four corners.

I remember the first time I felt beckoned by this tower. It was a sunny, late summer afternoon. My sister and I had been playing outside on the swingset most of the day. She had settled into the little TV room adjacent to our bedroom and I had settled onto her bed by the window.

My mother was in the kitchen on the phone as she was preparing something to eat. I could hear a pot on the stove, metal against metal. The water in the kitchen sink swooshed. The refrigerator door opened, and then closed.

I remember gazing up at the *box* and its four skinny antennae.

I can recall the experience of one of those steel arms reaching down for me as I sat at the bedroom window. In my memory, the WBAL tower bent down, the arm of one prong reaching all the way to my window. I climbed out my window and held on as the single prong carried me back up to the top of the tower. This was all in the imagination of a five-year-old little girl, but what I recall most poignantly is the overwhelming, tender love I felt surrounding me.

As long as we lived on Dupont Avenue in Baltimore City, the WBAL tower was a source of comfort. It was always watching over me. At night, the lights would blink, comforting me. During the day, my occasional reverie on my sister's bed would quicken my heart. The love I felt from the tower was so reassuring and comforting, and while it wasn't a secret, I never told a soul. This was the magical thinking of a little girl who hides the butterfly wing she found into the corner of her dresser drawer for safekeeping.

It took another fifty years for me to realize that was my first awareness of my Savior's courtship of me. He was wooing me, calling to me; and He was prodding me to gaze up to Him. Gaze up toward Him I did.

I know now that beckoning my attention in His direction was my Savior's way of teaching me to hear His voice. Why would He call me at such a tender age? My only explanation is that He must have designed me to hear Him, and He knew I would need Him to guide me out of the complex wasteland that would become my life.

From the ends of the earth I call to you, I call as my heart grows faint; lead me to the rock that is higher than I. For you have been my refuge, a strong tower against the foe.
Psalm 61:1-3 (NIV)

◆◆◆◆◆

We love each other because he loved us first.
1 John 4:19(NLT)

Jesus' love for us is like a hot ember planted within our hearts at conception. I tucked mine away for "safekeeping" for most of my life. Looking back, I wonder if my gnawing discontent was due to a yearning for something I couldn't have. Was it that innocent, childlike joy, and sweet contentment that is the seed of love for a family, or was it actually the love of Jesus that I tucked away and longed for?

Maybe God designed children's innocence for the purpose of knowing Him in all His purity and holiness. His touch on our souls and inside His Holy DNA are the secrets to an eternal craving. It's a yearning that only He can satisfy.

When I was in nursing school, I learned that there is a spot on the heart muscle called the sinoatrial node (SA). It initiates the electrical stimulus that is in charge of the heartbeat. This SA node is the natural pacemaker of the heart and is responsible for the initiation of the cardiac cycle (heartbeat) that our technology can detect by five to six weeks in utero. It spontaneously generates an electrical impulse, which conducts electricity throughout the heart. What a miracle! God has His forefinger on our hearts! It reminds me of the image of God touching life into Adam in the Garden of Eden on Michelangelo's Sistine Chapel. God is the reason the heart starts beating in the womb and remains beating until shortly after we die. His design is to cast His fingerprint on our hearts so that the memory of our union with Him compels us to return to His arms!

Then Christ will make his home in your hearts as you trust in him.
Your roots will grow down into God's love and keep you strong.
Ephesians 3:17 (NLT)

◆ ◆ ◆ ◆ ◆

In 1959, the year before my brother was born, my sister and I moved downstairs to our new bedroom. I was five years old and my sister was six. Our bedroom was a smaller room than before. But my sister and I were *best buds*, and we were now closer to the door to our backyard, so all was good in our eyes.

During this time, there was a life-altering incident.

My mother had returned home from her afternoon activities. I don't know where she had been, but Lee, our maid, babysitter, and surrogate mother, had been keeping an eye on us. Knowing my mother, she was most likely returning from a rendezvous with a man.

Without warning, she came into the small bedroom that my sister and I shared and began yelling. She opened the door to the tiny closet that my sister and I shared and began grabbing everything, throwing it onto the floor and the beds. She yelled about how messy our closet was. We both stood there, speechless and in utter shock, as she raged.

She never hit us. I don't even recall her directing her rage at us, but her display filled us with fear and awe. Then, she threatened to leave. She actually did leave. She yelled something but I can't remember her words. I was only five years old. I can still see the scene as she stormed out the kitchen door and vanished. My mother was suddenly gone!

I ran through the living room into the kitchen, looking for her. In horror, I realized my mother wasn't there. My sister was crying hysterically. In silence, I froze. This event lives in my memory with fresh, palpable recall as if it occurred only yesterday. It is imprinted deeply because that was the moment my deep bond with my sister developed a fracture.

I watched my terrified big sister, red-faced and sobbing wildly, and decided at that moment that my mother left us because she was only angry at her. In my young heart, I couldn't bear the thought that I had caused my mother to leave. I couldn't endure the thought that I was so bad that I'd made my mother that upset. In my feeble little child's mind, I made it my sister's fault.

The tragedy is that at that moment, I solidified within my heart the imperative that for the rest of my life, I'd never do anything to make my mother angry. It was the birth of a self-righteous walk I'd learn to master throughout the rest of my childhood and well into adulthood. Not until the humbling shame of my divorce from my first husband four decades later did I begin the slow dismantling of that self-righteous posture.

Even more tragic is the impact my distorted interpretation of that day had on my relationship with my soulmate older sister, whom I considered my BFF. She was my life. She was my joy and all the fun of childhood wrapped up in one person. The sun rose and set upon her, and the joy of summer days in fantasy play revolved around her creative, whimsical mind.

That tragic day began the dismantling of the sister love and easy companionship we had shared. It began an insidiously destructive comparison process which I'd used to measure my behavior with my parents against how my sister interacted with them. It became the foundation of tension and division that I wouldn't fully release myself from until well into the sixtieth year of my life. I lost the years of companionship in sisterhood with her as we drifted in and out of communication with each other. From the birth of our children through our failed first marriages and new remarriages, I could easily go months or years with little or no contact with her. It's one of the greatest losses of my life, and further fallout from my mother's indiscretions.

Looking back now, I realize my mother's rage had more to do with a failed rendezvous with her love interest at the time than her children's behavior or messiness. But, at the time, and well into my adulthood, I believed that she was angry at my sister and me. Decades later I was told that she never even left our property. She sat on the front porch step pouting and seething. Maybe it was due to a disappointment in a love encounter, or maybe it was her own shame at how she had behaved toward her children. Questions unanswered.

A person without self-control
is like a city with broken-down walls.
Proverbs 26:28 (NLT)

CHAPTER 3

Hidden Shame

Hear the word of the Lord, O people of Israel!
The Lord has brought charges against you, saying:
"There is no faithfulness, no kindness, no knowledge
of God in your land. You make vows and break them;
you kill and steal, and you commit adultery."
Hosea 4:1-2 (NLT)

As young children, we aren't able to fully understand or find the words to make sense of what the cherishing of our beloveds really means. We can't conceptualize the meaning of security or love. We are left instead with an ocean of feelings and yearnings.

Because the foundation of my life was built on lies and secrets, I wore inauthenticity and shame like a cloying wet shirt. It clung to my soul and seeped into my psyche. My search for relief from this is what ultimately led me to Jesus.

The ensuing journey of my life from childhood to adulthood revealed at first a love for a family that had no bounds. Joy and delight spiced my life, but over time, that childlike reverie became tainted, and it morphed into the compulsion to worship family. My family and my role within it became my idol. This set the pattern to a lifelong detour that guided me back to my Creator.

My first introduction into my mother's infidelity was when I was four or five years old. I believe my mother was actually kicked off the elementary school PTA, amid some scandalous references to the school principal. In retrospect, this was the beginning of my vague awareness of my mother's life of adultery and coquettishness.

We lived across the street from our elementary school. My mother had been volunteering there, usually at the nurse's office. I recall a particular evening when my mother returned home shouting, from what I now realize must have been the PTA meeting where they had kicked her off. I watched her yelling about it when she entered our house.

I can only piece together the scenario, based upon who my mother was. I still recall a sense of teachers' eyes following me and an awareness of what I can only identify now as shame when I'd walk down the halls of Edgecombe Elementary School. I strongly suspect that my beautiful, raven-haired mother was either flirting too much with the principal of my school or was having an affair with him. My mother stopped volunteering at my school shortly after that, so I'll never know for sure. I can only surmise based upon who she was, her rages at the time, and my vague sense of shame.

The abashment at the school ground property continued in other ways as I worked my way through all of my school years. These were the days in middle and upper school when I'd have an afternoon activity and needed to wait for my mother to pick me up at the end of the day. She was always late; very late. Oftentimes, I'd be the last human body on the school grounds when her car finally appeared racing into the parking lot. I recall sitting on the bench outside the school as even the principal left for the day. He'd stop to check on me and make sure I had a ride home. My shame was palpable.

◆ ◆ ◆ ◆ ◆ ◆

The dance of adultery that my mother chose was one that required her daughters to dance with her. We were her counselors when her heart broke or her anxiety peaked at an absent phone call. We were her targets when anxiety, fear, and rage overtook her when a relationship inevitably went wrong.

My mother was gentle with us. She never verbally abused us or hit us. However, she was unrelenting in her need for us to be the salve on her broken heart and the partner in her celebrations when her relationships were thriving. She was unpredictable in her moods, depending on the fluctuations of her extramarital affair at that time.

I was personally aware of and involved in five of her affairs. I've always suspected that there were more. My mother was proud of my sister and me. She loved to show us off to her men. My first introduction to one of my mother's lovers was around five years old. His name was John C. It was later that I learned he was my mother's therapist. He had blue eyes that sparkled with his kind smile. She brought us to his place of work once. I can only recall cigarette smoke and a large room full of men. I don't know if he was a counselor for veterans or a social worker. My memories are vague flashes of images.

I recall an afternoon when I was alone with my mother. I don't know where my sister was, but I suspect she was in kindergarten or first grade. My mom brought me to the home of John C. We climbed a stairway in a small apartment building. His place was at the top of the first landing. I can still see his broad, kind smile when he opened the door. There was a hallway with a living room off to the left. My mother sat me on the couch and put on the TV. I can recall the jovial banter between John and my mother. I was to sit and wait as I watched them going down the hallway to the back of the apartment, most likely to his bedroom.

I don't recall how long they left me alone, and I didn't venture out of the living room. Knowing me, it was because my mother told me not to. I always did what my mother told me to do, so I waited. They could have been gone five minutes or an hour. I will never know. But they were gone long enough for me to get restless, and for it to get the better of me.

I accidentally pushed a cigarette-filled ashtray onto the carpeted floor. The most vivid recollection I have is the panic I felt at five years old, trying to clean up my mess. I remember the looming guilt I felt when my mother came in and saw me rubbing black cigarette ash into the carpet.

The irony is that in my attempt to make the cigarette stain vanish from the rug, I was unintentionally creating a permanent mark. The sound of her agitation and anger at me echoed off the walls of that room, piercing my soul. The stain of that shame began to tangle its way firmly into my heart on that day.

✦✦✦✦✦✦

By the time I was thirteen, *the dye was cast*. When the normal teenager was hanging out at the local deli, I cuddled on the couch with my parents watching TV. When other kids were going to socials and dances, I was content to stay home with my mother and father. I played the piano in the living room beside my newspaper-reading dad. I gleaned as much contentment in pleasing him as he did in having me nearby. My social life consisted of one girlfriend who was even more introverted than me. Her parents were tattooed-bearing Jewish Holocaust survivors from Germany. As a result, she was also a girl who kept close to home. We were like two broken girls with clipped wings.

Staying close to home ensured my role in protecting my family from the misdeeds of my mother. If the phone would ring during our family time in front of the TV, I would be the one to answer. I would be the one to cozy up to my mother and whisper in her ear that "So-and-So is on the phone." She could demurely excuse herself from my father's side on the couch, where I could take her place; a surrogate wife of sorts. If my father was aware of what was going on in these moments, I'll never know.

This illusion of fulfillment and the false construction of my distorted identity continued until the event I refer to as *the final nail in the coffin of my life*. I was in my sophomore year of high school. I had managed to get selected to the JV cheerleading squad. In the 1970s, this was a very big deal. This was particularly momentous because I was never athletic. I was average to below average as a performer in gym activities. I was always one of the girls who were "last picked" for team sports.

In spite of this, when cheerleader tryouts came around, I had made a decision. I was obsessed with making it onto the squad. I desperately wanted the adoration and attention I believed I'd receive as a cheerleader. I'd finally feel seen in a life where I felt anything but visible. I began the herculean focus that became a hallmark of my personality. I was determined! From the moment I returned from school until it was dark outside, I practiced. In front of my mirror in my bedroom, I trained. While in bed, I practiced in my mind's eye. It was all-consuming.

In the end, they selected me for the JV squad in my sophomore year. Here I was, the girl whom kids would fight not to have on their Greek dodge team, a cheerleader at Randallstown High School! My enthusiasm and passion positioned me to become a captain of the varsity squad the following year. Everyone knew the cheerleading coaches had their eyes on me for the next captain post.

Then, my back went out. I began to have a vague discomfort in my upper thighs while sitting for long periods of time. That discomfort worked its way down to my ankles by the third period of my school day. This had been going on for several months before I said anything to my parents. By the spring of 1970, I was on an x-ray table in an orthopedic surgeon's office. I can still recall the cold metal table, the clinical, cold hands of the technician who ignored my tears as she positioned and repositioned my body to get the most accurate view of my spine.

The surgeon took one look at the x-ray and said to my mother that I would probably need spinal surgery. All I could hear was my voice interrupting him and demanding to know, "Can I still cheer?" His response was clear and resolute. It was a resounding, "No!" The glory days I yearned for as a cheerleader were, sadly, not meant to be. The only path to creating a healthier balance to my adolescence vanished with the surgeon's diagnosis.

The doctor called it spondylolisthesis, a slippage of the spinal column. This differs from the typical "slipped disc." My slipped vertebrae was at the L5/S1 level. The orthopedic surgeon abruptly stated that if I didn't have surgery, I was at risk of losing the ability to walk. He recommended a repeat evaluation in six months from then.

I sat and watched his lips move. I saw my mother's frowning brow and could see her asking questions. It was as if I couldn't hear anything. The only question I cared about was "Can I still cheerlead"? It was all that mattered to me because it was my only gateway out of the jailkeeper's role I had erected for myself with my parents. I didn't think of it in exactly that way at the time. I only felt like an oxygen tank was being pulled away from me in a room that had no air. In retrospect, had I been able to continue on the trajectory that cheerleading and leading the high school varsity squad would have offered me, I believe with some certainty that I would have experienced some normalcy as a teenager.

Instead, my remaining high school life, and in some ways my entire life, detoured onto a path that influenced my development as an adolescent and young adult. I began avoiding the lobby at the end of the school days because the cheerleaders would be practicing there. Shame and sorrow escorted me out the back door of the school.

Six months later, I was back on an x-ray table with a new orthopedic surgeon, seeking a second opinion. He took one look at the picture and scheduled a spinal fusion two weeks later. He indicated that if left untreated, I'd be a paraplegic in a very short time.

In the 1970s, the recovery process for a spinal fusion required the patient to lay flat on their back for two months. My parents rented a hospital bed, and I recovered in our family den at the opposite end of our house. I quietly worried that I'd never walk again. I was too uneducated about the human body at that point to understand that if I could move and feel my lower extremities, neurologically, I'd be fine.

Those two months in bed sealed my fate. My world became smaller. I no longer had to maintain the walls of my self-imposed restrictions. The doctor's instructions became a prescription for isolating myself. My recovering spine dictated the direction of my life from that point forward. It limited me physically and socially. I wore a brace for several months after the spinal fusion. Going to dances was out of the question. For the rest of high school I was excused from gym class.

I began to want to listen to classical music and was particularly drawn to Gregorian chants. I envisioned stained-glass church sanctuaries. Being Jewish, I have no explanation as to why I'd be drawn to the image of cloistered sanctuaries, yet I was.

Another result of surgery and recovery was that I decided I wanted to become a nurse someday. The nurses' *tender loving care* and focused attention on me was a balm to my defeated body and spirit. I identified with the nurses who cared for me in the hospital and wanted to be like them. As a junior in high school, I knew what my life was going to be. I would go to nursing school, become a nurse, eventually get married, have a family, then die. Beyond that, dreams and passion never made it onto my radar screen. As planned, I became a registered nurse, and I eventually married a man thirteen years my senior. We had two beautiful daughters. However, the marriage lasted only twelve years.

As the years passed, I'd refer to this passage of spinal surgery as the final nail in my coffin, a small box for the small life of a Jewish girl who had not yet met Jesus.

POCKETS OF PAIN

Sorrow dwells in crevices and alcoves of our soul.
Sometimes I'll curl up in one of those nooks and just be with it.
The sorrow exists because love gave it life.
It's searing.
And eyes burn.
Regret and despair are the offspring of love's broken promises.
He knows.
He is my Comforter.
He is my Forgiver.
He lifts me up and places my feet on solid ground
and lights my way in the darkness.

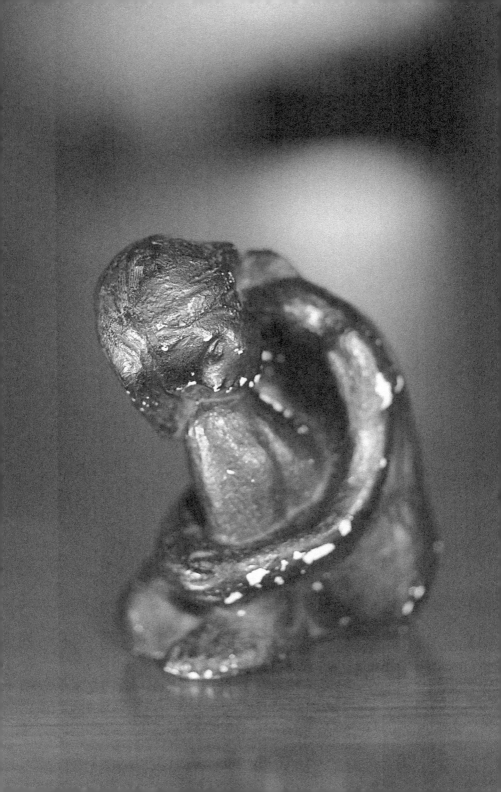

CHAPTER 4

It's A "Hurtin" Thing

Who is wise enough to count all the clouds? Who can
tilt water jars of heaven when the parched ground
is dry and the soil has hardened into clods?
Who provides food for the ravens when their young
cry out to God and wander about in hunger?
Job 38:37-38, 41(NLT)

I had a surrogate mother named Lee. One of her favorite sayings, when I was crying over something, was "it's a hurtin' thing." I use her phrase with my patients in my acupuncture treatment room to this present day. I can still feel Lee's powerful hugs as I'd nestle with teary eyes into the bosom of her strong embrace. She loved me powerfully, and I rested secure in that love my entire life. Lee knew my family's secrets and I know she hated them.

Lee would have been known to outsiders or guests in my home as our *maid*, as that was the term used in the 1950s through the 1970s. I knew her as my heart and my rock. As a young child, I thought she was the black woman in the picture of the Aunt Jemima on our pancake syrup bottle because she looked exactly like her. Lee, with her broad smile, booming voice, and cuddly hugs, was the consistent, reliable presence in our home that wobbled like a buoy in a storm. She was my lighthouse.

I can still recall her tuna fish salad sandwiches and smiles. She was the strong presence that reassured me that *all was right with the world*. Lee remained in my parents' employ for over twenty years. When my sister and I were little girls, Lee would send us on errands up the street to Wiley's, the tiny neighborhood grocery store, for that quick loaf of bread. Our special treat was when she sent us there for coddies on mustard. Coddies were ground up cod fish meat paddies, fried, and placed on Saltines with mustard. The cashier would wrap Lee's and tuck it into a brown bag. My big sister and I would eat ours on our walk back home. We'd compete with each other over who could eat the slowest, making the coddie treat last the longest.

Walking to Wiley's, like *two big girls*, on those warm, sultry summer days holds a sacred place in my memory. I recall balmy walks with my sister in Indian summers as we crunched through the colorful leaves on our mission to the corner store. We'd make acorn rings and play hopscotch for hours. The smells of fallen leaves on the sidewalk in autumn are savory imprints in my mind. These memories belong to Lee as well. She was as present as the rising sun.

Lee's imprint in my memory is indelible. My father hired her to work two to three days a week. It could have been every day early on—I don't recall exactly. I do recall that she was always home in the family room ironing with the television on when I'd return from school. While I could never predict if my mother would be home when I returned, I always knew that I'd find Lee there. She was my rock to stand on in the days of my youth.

My twenty-year addiction to the soap operas I attribute to Lee, because she always saved the ironing pile for the hours of the day where she could iron and watch the soaps simultaneously. Early on in 1970, Lee would iron beside my hospital bed in the family room as I recuperated from my spinal surgery. This memory is as comforting today as it was then.

There was a reassuring soothing that came with Lee's large-as-life personality. Due to my fragile frame and mind in those days, Lee's presence in my life is a loving memory that my heart refuses to relinquish.

In reflecting on my relationship with her, Lee was the person I could most be myself with. I felt her unconditional love. She *saw* me. My welfare mattered to her. My relevance mattered to her. I never felt shame and could ask her for things such as lunch or my bedpan in my spinal recovery days. Lee always treated me with integrity and love. When you feel fully accepted and loved by another person, you maintain a special cozy nook within your heart and mind dedicated solely to that person.

I have vague memories of shouting between my mother and her. Lee's anger was palpable but ineffectual in subduing the cravings of my mother's clandestine addictions. Looking back, I now understand that Lee knew, and it enraged her. In my heart, I know her rage was founded in her love for me and my two siblings. I believe she hurt for my father as well, who was helpless to change my mother's behavior.

When I finally received my driver's license at age sixteen, I'd volunteer to drive Lee to the bus stop. On days where she was running late, I'd volunteer to drive her all the way home. It simply felt like *the right thing to do*; not to mention that I loved my newfound freedom behind the wheel of my mother's car.

When my brother graduated from college, we took two cars and all drove up to Frostburg State College for the ceremony. I volunteered to drive Lee, who insisted on attending. I drove downtown to pick her up, and we set out for Western Maryland. Alone with Lee on that long drive was when I learned that my mother never left us on that tragic day in the kitchen. I don't recall that Lee was even there on that day. That was also when I learned that in the early years of her employment with my family, she had several times informed my father of her plans on quitting. She simply did not want to work for my mother and witness her careless behavior with the hearts of her husband and children. I learned that my father had begged her to stay. Lee quoted my father: 'because the children need you'. A sad and riveting revelation as to the weight of the addiction of my mother's philandering.

As a Christian, I look back on Lee's decision to stay with us as her loving sacrifice. She could have easily found other employment in those days, but she chose to stay with us. I know she was a Baptist, but at the time it meant nothing to me. While she is no longer alive for me to ask her, I choose to believe that she saw her work with my family as a ministry in parts. If she prayed for us, I will never know. What I do know is that her work and presence in our home was her act of prayer. It was her act of service to endure the presence of adultery for the sake of the hearts of the children that were beholden to her.

When I was pregnant with my first child nearly two decades later, I received a phone call from her daughter Robin. Lee had died and they set the funeral for the following day in downtown Baltimore. I attended. It was held at a Baptist church on North Avenue in downtown Baltimore, a black community in the heart of one of the many ghetto neighborhoods. I entered with my pregnant belly protruding as all eyes gazed at the lone white woman looking for a familiar face in the sanctuary. I sat beside her adult children Thomas, Robin, and Shirley. I marveled at the passion and waving hands of grief surrounding me. This was my first exposure to worshipping the Lord and reveling in the life of a fellow traveler.

I smile as I ponder that Lee is beaming as she looks down upon me now, knowing that we will reunite someday together in His kingdom. Lee was a blessing to me and she is the unsung heroine of my life story.

CHAPTER 5

But for the Love of Dad

*The Lord said to me, "Go and love your wife again,
even though she commits adultery with another lover. This
will illustrate that the Lord still loves Israel, even though the
people have turned to other gods and love to worship them."*
Hosea 3:1 (NLT)

It was a cold winter afternoon in 2016. My friend Elizabeth and
I were hunkered down in a cozy booth of a neighborhood coffee
shop chatting about my memoir manuscript. She asked me, "Jill,

you always talk about your mother and how she impacted your life, but you've never even mentioned your father. What's that all about?"

When she spoke those words, I received them like a conviction. There was no guilt. There was only the piercing notion in the center of my chest that a truth had just been spoken. I had no answer for her on that afternoon, and like a snooze alarm giving me extra time to drift along, I returned to the comfort of my busy, distracting life; but her words had set in motion another opening of my heart. It took me nearly six months to put a pen in hand to resurrect the legacy of my father.

It was time to turn to the memory of him. Who was he and what was his impact in this adulterous journey in my life? He died in 1984 at age sixty-two from complications of Parkinson's disease. His absence from my consciousness in the ensuing few decades spoke volumes, but I was clueless as to what any of those whispers meant. The fact that the words were inaudible was another problem. I'd have to turn to prayer and patience to allow it to be revealed in God's time and my willingness to hear it.

◆ ◆ ◆ ◆ ◆

In the summer of 2018, we had an unprecedented thunderstorm that devastated a nearby historic town and flooded my community like never before. Cars were literally floating downstream.

Our house did not escape the flooding, but the damage paled compared to other neighborhoods. The most serious problem we had was the fact that our basement stairwell had become clogged with leaves and had backed up, and water was pouring through the door jamb. My husband had to go outside in the storm and thunder to unclog the drain. I stayed inside with a pot, bucket, and broom. I monitored Larry and his precarious location as I alternated between trying to catch the water pouring in and sweeping water in the direction of the sump pump.

My six foot husband was chest deep in murky dark water in the vestibule and had to reach down to the drain. There was lightning with torrential rain outside. He tried to keep his head out of the water as he clamored and fumbled around attempting to clear the leaves and debris.

Groping through dark water is what it feels like, trying to rediscover who my father was and where my grief or disappointment about him were hiding. What I thought was a deep and abiding love for my father resulted in my showing up empty-handed. How is it I had become so completely detached about memories of my father? I loved him dearly, yet nothing emerged from my consciousness since his death. There was an eerie absence of feeling about it, and the silence was suddenly deafening.

I was about eighteen at the time my forty-six-year-old father was diagnosed with his illness. The diagnosis devastated him. He knew there was no cure, and the side effects he experienced from medications limited his ability to manage his illness. He contracted into his sorrow over his fate with in incurable disease and an adulterous wife. In many respects, that is when I lost my father.

Looking back now at the age of sixty-four, I realize that I didn't know my father very well. I hold on dearly to the memories of his tender heart and his abiding love for me. I still carry within my heart his loyalty to his family and his devotion to us all. My memories of the family trips and barbecues I attribute to my father. I attribute my love of gardening to the memory of shadowing my father as he landscaped our new home in Baltimore County. The late-night movies in front of the family TV, with his "double-decker" sandwiches on rye bread, are savory highlights of my life. I remember his famous egg salad sandwiches and milkshakes, and me practicing the piano while he sat on the couch reading the paper beside me.

As the years progressed, by 1984, my father's condition had rendered it necessary to have twenty-four-hour care and supervision, so he had to be hospitalized for eventual transfer to a nursing home. Because my mother had decided to separate from him a few years prior and he lived alone, there were no other options for him. This hospitalization devastated him. I'll never forget the afternoon during that last hospitalization when I went to visit him. He looked at me and said, "I think I have brain damage." My only response as I tried to hold back tears was, "I'd give my right arm to take that away from you, Dad." These were the words he always said to me when I'd come to him in distress over something as a little girl. I sat there with him, holding him and rocking him as he used to do with me in years past. The next day he suffered a stroke and was transferred to a long-term VA facility, where he died twenty-four hours later. I did not make it to his bedside in time. On December 7, 1984, my father died depressed and alone and I've regretted this my entire adult life.

I married my first husband four months after my father's death. We had had a long courtship and had finally become engaged in the summer of 1984. My mother intended to bring a married man she was having an affair with to my wedding and reception. I told her that if she insisted on bringing a guest, then she could not come to my wedding. In setting that boundary, I was protecting the memory and integrity of my father. By choice, I walked myself down the aisle in honor of him. There was no one who could or would take my father's place.

As I reflect, groping through the muddy waters of my memories, I'm left with only snippets of the man who married my mother. I believe that my father lived in silent sorrow. His own father, whom I never met, was a taxi cab driver and was held up at gunpoint and shot. I don't know the age of my father at that time, but I know that his father eventually died from complications of that injury.

In nursing school, when I was twenty years old, they required us to create a family genealogy tree. We were to interview as many family members as possible. My father and my aunt responded to my inquiries about my grandfather with a near-violent refusal to discuss the man. All they were willing to reveal was that he was an abusive alcoholic.

Today, I ponder how my father navigated his way throughout adolescence and adulthood, never having experienced the love and guidance from his father. I can only speculate on how challenging life was for my dad when he missed out on the foundation and strength that a good enough father can offer a son. I wonder if he received any mentoring or guidance from other father figures. Being raised as a Jew without a devout relationship to God, my father did not have guidance from a life built upon a foundation of biblical principles. Never having known Jesus, he was left to his own resilience and fortitude. Having no relationship with the only enduring shepherd, Jesus, I can only imagine what life was like for him. Having found Jesus late in my own journey, I am reminded every Sunday during worship time the former prison of my life, and because of this, my heart aches for my father.

Despite the absence of a father in his life, I marvel at how he managed to work his way through college, develop a career as a teacher, and later become a very successful insurance agent. I recall how his insurance clients would seek counsel on personal matters from him. My father was loved by so many people.

He enlisted in the Army Reserve after the attack at Pearl Harbor in 1941 and navigated fighter planes in the Asian Military Campaign. His squadron was actually scheduled to bomb Japan, but they called the attack off because of the bombing of Hiroshima.

He joined the brotherhood in our local synagogue. He ran for city council in the 1960s and lost to William Donald Schaefer, who became one of the most beloved mayors of Baltimore City decades later. My father supported his ailing sister and mother. While he was the *baby* and the only boy in his family, he filled the shoes that his own father had abandoned long before the gunshot wound.

My father was born into an era that did not indulge in emotions or sorrows. The era of *feelings* came in the 1970s and beyond. Was my father the last of the generation of *real men*, or was he a wounded and broken human being like the rest of us? I can only ponder what sadness and sorrow he endured, as he did so silently. He never spoke of his heartbreak over the lack of a father to lean on and gain strength from. He didn't know Jesus. My father lived his spiritual life alone, as far as I can tell. Like Hosea in the Old Testament, and the adulterous wife, my father endured an unrequited love with my mother.

It was in the wee hours of the night when as a young girl, my ears would witness his rage at my mother and her indiscretions. Those were the nights I'd lay in my bed across the hall from them with my pillow over my head, attempting to shut out the agony of their marriage. I'd remember worrying if they'd start fighting if a friend was in the house visiting me. I could hear them arguing sometimes when I had a playmate outside. How I hated other people bearing witness to the evidence of my fraudulent life.

Looking back now, as an adult, I realize that my father suffered his own burdens and sorrows silently. His grief over enduring the Great Depression, an abusive, abandoning father, and an adulterous marriage were his cross to bear.

However, despite all that, my recollection of my father was that of a man of integrity. He was honest and tenderhearted, devoted and reliable. My father was a responsible and conscientious provider to his family. He was a quiet man who loved his children and took pride in his home. He adored me, and I knew it. How I wish he knew Jesus!

***

In December 2016, I had to undergo surgery to an old injury of my right foot. Twenty years of wear and tear had set the stage for extensive arthritis there. My surgeon explained that the arthritis in my toe joint was so extensive that it hollowed out its center. He said that chronic arthritis, when left unchecked, will eventually destroy a joint. He described it like an *atomic bomb had exploded* inside. Maybe a hollow joint is like the vacuous hollow space in the foundation of a person's soul when life's sorrows take hold without release.

Since my father did not know Jesus and had what appeared

like only a shallow relationship with God, I have to conclude that my father did what most non-believers do: he used the will God gifted him with to do life on his own. Instead of growing up with a strong, loving father, he endured an abusive man instead. Perhaps this created the foundation that set the stage for Dad to attach himself to a woman who was deeply flawed. Maybe he had hollow spaces within himself that influenced his choice in a partner. They were two broken and wounded individuals who did the best they could. For me, growing up in a home that was permeated with adultery, deception, and unrequited love set the stage for my own hollow foundation, not unlike my arthritic toe joint.

My parents' crippled marriage and my mother's indiscretions broke my heart. Somewhere along that trajectory, I simply shut down. I developed the ability to stop feeling sorrow over it all, and I intellectualized everything. I mastered the ability to not feel. In 2000, I became an acupuncturist, and I've had acupuncture patients describe the detachment from their feelings when on antidepressants. I learned how to do that for myself without medication. The tragedy is that in the process, I lost touch with my father after his death. It was effortless and unconscious.

I only knew him as a child. He detached and contracted into his own Parkinsonian-fraught sorrow before I had a chance to learn about the man as an adult. I didn't get the chance to acknowledge his strengths along with his weaknesses that we as humans all have to balance. His ability to express his unconditional love and support of me was short-circuited when I was eighteen. I can only imagine what it might have been like to walk together in his twilight years as his daughter, knowing him and loving him on a shared journey together.

✦ ✦ ✦ ✦ ✦

Recently, after writing this passage, I was sitting on a bench at the lake. My second husband, Larry, our daughters, and I had been on a week's vacation and this was our last morning. Larry was inside packing and I walked down to the lake for one last view. Maybe it was the peace of the moment. Or maybe it was the first breath of the approaching winter upon my face? The lake was as still as glass. A lone crane perched on the dock, and a distant goose was crying out for its mate. Suddenly, for the first time since his death, I allowed myself to imagine my father. In my mind, he appeared out of nowhere and walked toward me. In my mind, I ran toward him and thrust myself into his outstretched arms. As he held me, all I could do was sob. These were the grieving sobs of a daughter who had lost her father too young. I cried out, "It's been so hard, Dad! It's been so hard! I've worked so hard to be good! I tried so hard! I missed you so much!" I envisioned him holding me and him kissing me on the head, telling me how proud he was of me.

There it was! I had hidden my love and grief over my father within the shadows of one of the many cozy nooks of my soul; the ones where I would hide my shame, sorrow, or anger throughout my life prior to knowing Jesus. I saw Dad, and the surge of yearning that exploded from my heart flooded my world. My father holding me with his strong, loving embrace was all there in that moment. The urgent need for him to know how tough my life had been without him was searing. The longing to share my love for him was overwhelming. My love and my need for my father were there all along.

As the vision faded, I sat on the bench and quietly continued to cry. I wiped my wet, salty face from the tears that held his memory. I knew I had to go back into the house to help Larry continue with our packing to go home, but instead, I lingered in the space that belonged to my father and me. How I needed to feel his strength! From his strength, I could have navigated my life with more ease and less fragility.

But this was not to be. The trajectory of our lives evolved very differently. My father was stoic in his silent sorrow. He was integrity personified. My father was tenderhearted and loving to his children. He was devoted and loyal in his role as head of household.

However, he was not capable of setting limits on my mother's meanderings. Maybe like so many other men, he was too mesmerized by her voluptuous beauty and he didn't want to snuff out that tantalizing glow. Perhaps he really was deeply in love with her.

I wonder if he knew that as a father in the 1960s if he divorced her, he'd lose custody of his children and not be able to offer us any protection at all. Maybe his foundation had hollowed out like my arthritic foot, rendering him too weak to push back on the adulterous wave that smothered our lives. I'll never know for sure what reality was for him.

If I had any anger toward him over the years, it might be in his inability to control my mother and put a stop to her adultery. I could choose to conclude that he did not protect me as a father should. This victim mentality is such a narrow and slippery emotional slope. It can become an addiction that can cripple a person's capacity to become his or her best self. I realize now, late in life, that these particular conclusions and ponderings would hold me back from becoming the person God designed me to be. These wonderings are the cornerstones of stories I've defined myself by. The seduction of victimhood is a temptation that presents itself continually in life. The tragedy of this mentality is that it keeps us in emotional and relational bondage. We are not free to love well or manifest the particular gifts that God designed within us.

When a family's existence is built upon the sand of deceit and lies, a child's capacity to develop a strong sense of self becomes severely disrupted. There is nothing of value to root her identity into. If the value of family, marriage, and parenthood are maligned by manipulation and immorality, a child's development and ensuing life journey become vulnerable. Neurotic and wounded patterns of behavior at best and addictions or violence at worst will result. Either way, the trajectory of a child's development is challenged.

In clamoring and groping in that dark, muddy water of my memory and soul, I'm left with stories I've created around the drama that unfolded in my family. By the grace of God and with the guidance of Jesus and his Holy Spirit, I'm beginning to see the landscape beyond my own shallow view. My stories have truth, yes; but they are only mine. They are not my father's. They are not even my grandfather's. In recounting these painful memories, I am struck by how small my own story really is. It's one small view of a landscape of so many lives that preceded mine.

As I record all of this, I remain convinced that my mother never set out to deliberately hurt her children or her husband. She was not evil. She was just tragically flawed and stuck in the mind and heart of an adolescent girl who never grew up or took responsibility for the relationships that were beholden to her.

Every person's life story has limitations. Holding on to my story to define myself is limiting me to one perspective only; one view of a history of a lineage of people who have tried to live their lives as best they could. These histories and legacies are the backdrops that are ours alone. They are the "cards dealt." We have a choice of how to carry them into our own journey…or if we want to carry them at all. We all have hollow spaces etched into the foundation of our souls. The challenge of our lives is to find the path that leads us to clarity and strength, and a capacity to love well.

CHAPTER 6

Wet Kisses

Let your favor shine on me. In your unfailing love,
rescue me. Don't let me be disgraced, O Lord,
for I call out to you for help.
Psalm 31: 16-17(NLT)

My parents separated for the second time in my life in 1966 when I was about twelve years old. My father moved out of the house and into a neighborhood in downtown Baltimore called Bolton Hill. I remember visiting my father and looking out from his balcony from the eighth floor at the construction below on Park Avenue. There was construction underway for a community that would become Bolton Place. Ironically, Bolton Place would become the location of my first married life and of my initiation into motherhood. I lived there from 1985 to 2004, enduring a tumultuous and volatile marriage for nearly twenty years.

When my parents separated I resided with my mother and my siblings in our family home in Randallstown in Baltimore County. It was a difficult year because of my father's absence. What stands out most poignantly is one particular evening that winter when my mother had been out on a *date*. I recall it as a double date with my widowed aunt and a man she was seeing. I was still awake in my bed when I heard their car come up the driveway. Voices and laughter erupted as they exited the car to come into the house. I jumped out of bed to peek out the window.

As I write this passage, my throat is tightening. I can still feel the shame that had moved in and taken up residence inside my twelve-year-old mind. With the sounds of them coming up the sidewalk, my heart beat faster and harder in my chest. I didn't understand it, but I was excited. I had come to like John C. very much. Recall, I had spilled the ashtray debris onto his rug years earlier in his apartment. My mother had apparently remained in a relationship with him; or had rekindled the relationship after my father moved out of the house. I felt his fondness for me and it drew me toward his kindness. I also recall thinking of him as handsome.

John made me feel special. While I was only twelve years old, my hormones were beginning their cascade of permutations. With my father gone, the mixture of excited anticipation and longing for the loving hugs I'd get from John only underscored my confusion and the array of contradictory images and feelings that defined that era of my life.

My father was absent, and there was another man in the house. These confusing feelings shaped the direction of my sexuality and my identity well into my adulthood.

I jumped back into bed and under the covers. My heart was pounding hard against my chest. I could hear my mother and aunt and their *guests* laughing and talking down the hall from my bedroom. My mother must have come into my room to say good night. I don't recall if I asked my mother to let him come in or she offered to send him to my room. But Mr. C came into my room to *tuck me in* that night. I recall him cuddling in bed with me. I remember him holding me close, spooning me. If there was sexual tension at that moment, I don't recall. I only know that somewhere later in the week, I confided to my mother that I didn't like Mr. C's *wet kisses*.

Fast forward twenty-two years when I was about thirty-four years old. I'm in bed with my first husband in our Bolton Place townhouse. For the umpteenth time in several months, I've experienced the same sense of panic and anxiety as he approaches the bed for the night. My throat tightens, and my heart is banging in my chest. There is a sense of dread and oppression that makes no sense. I'd often pretend I was asleep to avoid any physical contact, or I'd read a book with a dim nightlight.

During this particular time, I had stumbled upon an autobiography called *The Words to Say It*. It was about a woman who had grown up in the inner city, enduring years of abuse and neglect. I was reading about her account of a near-rape in the stairwell of her apartment building, and I was unaware at the time that her story would unlock my own memory.

While I was driving to work later that week, and after I had finished reading that book, I was struck with the recollection of Mr. C in my bed that winter night long ago. Until that moment twenty-two years later, I had never thought about it. But as I drove down Route 70 on the way to work, the memory came flooding back. I had to pull over to the side of the road to catch my breath as I cried. Words failed me. There were only heaving sobs and an aching head. The shame was too dark; the emotions too raw.

As I recounted the incident to my therapist after work that afternoon through sobs and hiccups and crying, I was freeing myself of something I never even knew I had trapped within. To this day, fifty years later, I do not recall the details of any actual sexual assault. There was no penetration. I'm not sure he did anything to me other than cuddle with me and give me *wet kisses*. Mr. C made me feel special and that was all that mattered. But in my twelve-year-old girl's mind, heart, and body, it was still taboo and wrong and shameful, yet simultaneously exhilarating and wonderful.

It was filled with desire and deception and disloyalty to my father; secrets and fear as well as disgust. It was the embodiment of shame. I was too young to know any better and at the same time, old enough to know better; an existential conundrum that no one would protect me from. My father had moved away, and my mother was too wrapped up in herself to notice the difference or to protect me from Mr. C. or from myself.

My therapy session ended with me emotionally spent. I went home feeling relieved, with a sense of freedom I hadn't realized had been absent from my life. The panic and dread that I felt when my husband approached the bed never returned.

If only that had been the sole mountain I'd have to scale. Little did I know, this was only the beginning.

CHAPTER 7

Reality Check

"For I know the plans I have for you," says the Lord.
"They are plans for good and not for disaster,
to give you a future and hope."
Jeremiah 29:11 (NLT)

My role as my mother's daughter ran so deeply and shaped me so insidiously that had I not entered psychotherapy in 1979 at age twenty-five, I'm certain I'd have followed in my mother's footsteps. One afternoon early in my psychotherapy journey, I recall entering my therapist's office in a very agitated state. For about four months, I had been dating the man who was to become my first husband.

I cried to my therapist I was going to hurt this man and his nine-year-old son. I knew that it was only a matter of time before I'd have an affair. My therapist looked aghast and asked a simple question: "Is there another man that you are interested in?" I replied, "Of course not," but I knew that, "In time there would be."

What followed was one of the most impactful reality checks of my entire life. He simply said to me, "Jill, just because your mother did it doesn't mean you have to do it!"

He broke a spell with those words! It was as if someone had just lifted a mountain off my shoulders. I gazed at him in wonder. The relief was immediate. What is most striking about this event was that at the time, I appeared to have my life totally together to anyone on the outside looking in. I had recently graduated from a bachelor's level nursing program and was working in the intensive care unit at

Johns Hopkins Hospital in Baltimore. I was an independent woman who had my own apartment and my own car.

My level of confusion and distortion about my life and how I related to it was imperceptible. If anyone delved deeper in an attempt to get to know me, they would have seen past the young nurse who lived in the apartment upstairs and discovered my narrow social life and bouts of depression. I had very few friends and spent the majority of my time alone. In 1979, I even took a three-month backpack trek through Europe by myself. I recall a young Canadian commenting on the wall he could sense around me. I was painfully insecure socially and my default was to maintain a level of distrust of women, which short-circuited any possibility of deep friendships with them.

Having men as friends was not something I'd even attempt to approach. However, dating men and becoming intimate made me feel like the woman I didn't really believe I had the right to be. Sexual relatioships validated my identity as a woman. These brief relationships were shallow at best. I was incapable of looking a man in the eye or playfully flirting with any intention at the time.

My mother's sexuality and promiscuity seeped into my soul and competed for space with my identity as a woman. In my conflict about her sexuality and the sense of shame and *dirtiness* I had about it, I also felt overshadowed by her dominant role as my mother. Sexuality and womanliness were her birthrights, which left no room for me to discover mine in any healthy or balanced way.

My womanliness felt like it placed me in direct competition with my mother. Being the obedient *good girl* that I was, I felt only a superficial sense of confidence in my attractiveness. I felt chronically competitive with other women, which contributed to my mistrust of them and limited my ability for deep, lasting female friendships. Intimacy with men was my only avenue to solidifying any sense of womanliness, which I deeply wanted. It left me empty and unfulfilled beyond my short-termed sense of confidence.

◆◆◆◆◆◆

This competitiveness with other women began in early adolescence. When I was about thirteen years old, I was in the passenger seat with my mother driving me somewhere. It was a hot summer day, and the windows were open because our car did not have air conditioning in those years. I was wearing my first pair of sunglasses that were the hot style back then. They were large glasses with black frames and a kelly-green design. We were at a red light when I noticed a man standing on the corner gazing into our car. In my naiveté and a newly budding sense of *sexiness* about myself in my new sunglasses, I thought he was looking at me. The instant I felt his gaze, and I interpreted it as looking at me, I felt a deep sense of guilt because *I* was being noticed, rather than my mother.

The thought of outshining or competing with her was so alarming that I had to look away. And there it was; the beginning of my inability to look a man in the eye with any sense of confidence. The guilt and shame were becoming so deeply ingrained into my psyche that it took decades before I could begin deliverance from them.

Looking back, I'm sure that man on the sidewalk was actually noticing my mother through the rolled-down window on that hot summer day. In fact, it wouldn't be surprising if he was looking in our direction because my mother had made eye contact with him first. What is striking is the profound sense of guilt I felt at the possibility of subsuming the flirtations and attractions of men I believed were my mother's birthright, not mine. While I have finally been freed of that unspoken command of my mother's, the shame I felt at the possibility of usurping her birthright back in the summer of 1967 is palpable to this day.

It took nearly another forty years before I'd be able to look a man in the eye. To look directly at a man and to make eye contact, with the intention of simply doing so, eluded me until July 3, 1999. That was the night I met the blue-eyed man who would eventually become my cherished second husband, Larry.

CHAPTER 8

Miracle at Montebello

Though I am the least deserving of all God's people,
he graciously gave me the privilege of telling the Gentiles about
the endless treasures available to them in Christ. I was chosen to
explain to everyone this mysterious plan that God, the Creator
of all things, had kept secret from the beginning.
Ephesians 3:8-9 (NLT)

Sometimes God will use even the sinners who do not yet personally know Him to intercede for him to help another human being.

It was the fall of 1989. I recall the season because I was pregnant with my first child, and I was still working full time as a nurse consultant at a rehab facility in northern Baltimore City. My role was to support the nurses working with trauma patients and to offer psychiatric support to the patients as well. They sent many of the patients to Montebello Hospital from the University of Maryland Shock Trauma unit. I would always say, "You don't end up in rehab without emotional consequences. Rehabilitation from whatever cause is difficult at best and devastating at worst."

It was the end of the day, and I was making my rounds to my assigned patients. It was Friday, and I was eager to go home and put my tired feet up. The last patient I checked on was the one I wanted to visit the least. She was an obese woman in her seventies who had suffered a stroke. She had been in our facility for about two weeks. She was what we in the field would often refer to as a *train wreck.*

They had assigned me her case because the staff thought she suffered from depression. One of the things that made her so difficult for the staff as well as for me was that she was barely verbal. It was not like I could sit and chat with her in order to find a way to offer support.

She had been living with her elderly brother in a narrow row home in Baltimore City with a steep staircase leading to the second-floor bedroom. Going home was a poor option, to say the least, but going home was her only wish. Since case reviews had evolved to determine discharge dates as deemed appropriate by an outside insurance company, the needs of the patients usually took a backseat to the demands of the insurance system.

The hospital had determined that she had reached her fullest potential, and that rehab was no longer appropriate or justifiable. Since her few words were consistently "go home," they slated her for discharge the following day.

When I first met her, we spoke very few words. I introduced myself and would briefly sit with her. I was an advocate for her care with bedside nursing recommendations in staff meetings, but my input into her life was minimal. She was not challenging or interesting. She was just *there*.

I had been nursing for about fourteen years at this point in my career. I was proud of my work and my commitment to my patients. This patient, however, challenged my professional self-esteem, because as I prepared to walk into her room for the last time, I had to admit to myself that I had failed her. I knew she shouldn't be discharged. I knew her death was a guarantee and that it would be ugly. She'd probably die in her own excrement, neglected and alone.

I had not advocated for her by insisting that we override the demands of the insurance company or protocol. I could have done that. Nor had I advocated keeping her at Montebello so she could die with dignity. Discharging her home was going to be tragic. I knew it, and I had done nothing to fight against it. My reluctance to walk into her room late that Friday afternoon resulted from my guilt at failing to intervene on her behalf.

I entered the room and sat in a chair about ten feet from her. I didn't even tell her I was there. She appeared to be asleep, if not unconscious. I only wanted to finish my work and intended to stay briefly. She was to be discharged the next morning and I wanted to leave the guilt behind and let her be, so that when I returned on Monday, she'd be gone and I could pretend she never happened. God had other plans.

As I sat there, I began to feel the weight of my own body. I attributed it at first to my second-trimester pregnancy and the fatigue of a long week. I'm not sure how much time had gone by, possibly fifteen minutes, when the hospital clergyman and his assistant walked in to do rounds. He nodded at me and walked over to the sleeping woman and prayed over her. I don't recall the prayer, but it was a prayer that sounded familiar to me.

He left with another nod to me, and there I sat. I felt increasingly restless to leave the room but became acutely aware of feeling a weight upon my shoulders, as if I were being held down. I literally felt unable to lift myself off the chair. Time ticked by. It felt as if an hour passed, when suddenly out of the silence, the patient spoke. Without turning her head in my direction and with her eyes still closed she said, "Jill, I can't go home tomorrow. I'm too sick." I didn't think she was even aware that I was in the room! To say I was shocked is an understatement. I jumped out of my chair and ran over to her bedside and hugged her, promising her I'd take care of it.

I was euphoric as I literally ran down the hall to the doctor's office. I told him he had to cancel the discharge order because she requested to stay. My euphoria was on her behalf, but even more powerful was the experience of being involved in God's work. I was not yet a *believer*. I considered myself to be *spiritual*, but I had no personal relationship or intimacy with God. He had used me nevertheless, and I knew it!

When I returned on Monday, she was gone. She had died that weekend in her clean hospital bed, with peace and with dignity. I'd often wonder if the vigil I had felt required to perform that Friday afternoon had actually provided the space for her to reconcile her life to God, and allow herself to die. It was one of many miracles to come.

This amazing incident was tucked away somewhere in my mind as I ventured on from that day. Five months later, I became the mother of a little girl—and four years later to another daughter as well. My nursing career ended with the birth of my first child. My marriage struggled on as I tried to be the best mother and wife I could.

A neighbor's home was getting painted and I recall one of the painters outside my house say to me, as he watched us all walk through the front door, "the perfect family." His words pierced my emotional armor and went straight to my heart. The target he hit was my secret; that the image of my perfect family was a lie. Beyond that awareness, I still had no solution, so I tucked this away as well into one of my many nooks that concealed all my sorrows.

CHAPTER 9

End of an Era

For God, who said, "Let light shine out of darkness,"
made his light shine in our hearts to give us the light of the
knowledge of God's glory displayed in the face of Christ.
2 Corinthians 4:6 (NIV)

My first husband's temper and controlling nature assured my inability to truly open my heart to him. He was exquisitely intuitive, and I'm sure he sensed this about me. As a result, he'd grow angrier and more frustrated with me. This vicious cycle sustained itself from 1985 to 1998, for nearly thirteen years until we separated.

It was June 1998, and it was God's grace and mercy that finally shattered my defenses, which allowed me to see the hopelessness of my marriage. There had been a series of verbal outbursts from my husband about my inadequacies as a wife and a mother. They were occurring with more frequency. One particular night, I could not fall asleep. I lay there the entire night, as God began whispering to me in earnest. At the time I did not realize it was Him, but reflecting on that night I have no doubt His breath was upon me.

That sleepless night, in the wee hours of the morning, I eventually relinquished control. I allowed Him to reveal to me what I had refused to see. At last, I could see my marriage, and family life, and the effect it was having on my daughters with such crystal clarity that inaction was no longer an option. With the removal of the barrier from my ears, I could ultimately hear His words: "This is wrong.

This is harming your children. You are valued." These were the initial whisperings I heard that night.

It was five A.M in the morning when I got out of bed and called my sister. I woke her up because I needed to declare it to someone. When she asked me what was wrong, I told her I couldn't do this anymore. I told her I had finally realized that I had as much value under this roof as my husband. Her words were prophetic as they reached my heart. "Thank God...you've seen the light. You'll never go back into the darkness."

With my eldest daughter eight years old and my youngest nearly four, I was ready to *hear* God whisper to me. I was ready to take action. Had I not been a mother, I can only wonder if I'd ever have allowed the Lord to remove the blinders. Acknowledging the impact the tumultuous marriage was having on my daughters was the impetus I needed.

I wonder if my husband's outbursts toward me were a reaction to my inability to love him deeply, or at all. He must have sensed it, but I was clueless. I saw myself as the victim, the martyr. It was over a decade later within the embrace of my second marriage that I found the safety and space to begin to see myself more clearly. I began to understand and learn where my challenges were as a wife and lover. It was only by going through the journey in a safe space with my second husband that I began to learn to love a man in a substantive way.

But on that night in 1998, without my realizing it, I had set the stage for a new era in my life. On that sleepless night, God whispered, and I finally listened. The scales over my eyes dropped away as well. He illuminated my inner vision so I could see with acute clarity the brokenness of that marriage and the impact it was having on my daughters. As dawn broke that morning, I lay there gazing out into the thin sheet of light that peered from beyond the window shade. I heard my own voice in my mind. It said, "You'd suffer less as a single mom than as a married mom." What followed was a statement I whispered to myself that revealed the long journey in front of me. "You don't deserve to suffer this much. You're not that bad of a person."

It took nearly another decade before I would allow Jesus to finally step in and take all the suffering from me, because in His mercy and His grace, He didn't want me to suffer at all.

My first husband and I were finally divorced in September 2000. While the papers were signed, the agony of that marriage dragged into the divorce situation with a number of revisits to lawyers and the court system. It wasn't until 2006 that those legal battles in life would finally end. The emotional and financial consequences reverberated painfully for years to come. This was an unfortunate outcome for both my daughters and a real challenge to my second marriage in the first several years.

MY WEAKNESS, HIS MERCY

In my weakness, I will boast, because that is where God met me.
Thank you, Lord!
It is He who lifted me out from my darkness and into the light.
My story is about my weakness and God's mercy.
It's a story of brokenness,
A life dominated by pride.
I could never have found His pasture on my own in such a state.
He led me there.
He protected me.
He whispered into my heart: Live…live…love.

CHAPTER 10

A *Swaddling Moment*

His left hand is under my head,
and his right hand embraces me!
Song of Songs 2:6 (NLT)

There have been moments where the presence of God in my life was undeniable. Whether it was in a touch, or a conviction, or a physical gift; His presence moves me deeply. Describing such moments is not unlike trying to describe a color; or to describe the taste of something without using an adjective. How does a person completely describe who God is? It's like trying to contain a palm full of seawater, or reaching for a cloud or trying to describe a dream as you become fully awake. Pastel images without a canvas.

One of the most striking moments was late one night in the spring of 2002. I had been managing life in the single motherhood world for about three years at this point. I was lying in my bed trying to fall asleep. Suddenly, I felt something softly wrapping around my legs. The sensation was so palpable that I had to look down at my legs. Even as I record this incident, I question if it was a dream or reality. Maybe it was both?

The presence of this blanketed wrapping sensation continued up my legs and toward my waist. It felt as if I were being swaddled by a loving parent. The love was all-encompassing, warm and sweet.

Again, I looked and saw no one. Nothing.

But, what was undeniable was the sudden awareness of love as soft as a baby's blanket. The warmth and enveloping were palpable and profoundly humbling. All I could do was gaze in its direction as if someone was standing over me at the foot of my bed.

Who was this? What was this? Was it an angel wrapping its wings around me, embracing me?

On some level, I knew it was Him. I knew it was God…maybe Jesus. This was prior to Jesus even being on my radar screen. These were my *all roads lead to God* days. These were the times of my self-righteous days, where my attempt to define myself as *okay enough* was still dictated by my attachments to my labels and comparisons to other people.

Yet, I remember silently hoping that it was Jesus.

Why would you love me? These were the whisperings from my heart. I recall the sense of unworthiness, and I was so profoundly humbled by His presence that the weight of my unworthiness forced me to look away.

It was another two years before I began to gaze in the direction of Jesus with intention. Two years is a long time in worldly terms. Maybe for Jesus, time is another form of intelligence beyond my meager mind's ability to grasp. Maybe on this particular moment in God's eternity, He stepped in to swaddle me with His love, because He knew I was on the precipice of turning toward His son. He knew even before I did.

I marvel at how Jesus is always present beside us even when we are not looking for him. I'm astonished at his relentless presence as He readies himself to assume full residence within our hearts and minds.

So humble yourselves under the mighty power of God,
and at the right time he will lift you up in honor.
Give all your worries and cares to God,
for he cares about you.
1 Peter 5:6-7(NLT)

NOTHING IS HIDDEN FROM YOU

Peaceful and pure.
Muted sounds, a chime.
Soft whispers.
Birds' sweet words.
Man's creations and work, a distant echo.
God's breath in slow motion.
Soft dewy mornings after the storms.
One continuous, cleansing sigh.

CHAPTER 11

Point of Contact

And he will startle many nations, Kings will stand speechless
in his presence. For they will see what they had not been told;
they will understand what they had not heard about.
Isaiah 52:15 (NLT)

To meander through life, broken and wounded within, and to unbeknownst to anyone else find my way into the arms of Jesus, is truly a stunning love story. It is a holy romance in its intimacy. No one discipled me. Until the year before I was reborn at the age of fifty-five, no one even evangelized to me. There were no Christian neighbors for me to model or be *jealous* of, or drawn to.

It was only Him and me and His whisperings and revelations. It was His way of developing, ever so slowly, my appetite for Him. Like appetizers before a great feast, they whet the appetite so we want more. They stimulate a deeper craving. Jesus wanted me to turn to Him with all of my heart, and I finally did.

As I tried to navigate my way through my former life without Jesus, God would *meet me* in miraculous moments. I look back on these moments as markers in the sand. Like breadcrumbs on the path He placed me on. When my faith or hope takes a *wobble*, I recall these moments when His presence along my journey was undeniable.

There was a life-altering moment four to five years before I actually began a deeper search for God and accepted Christ into my life. It was midnight somewhere around 2003 when I *heard* a voice inside my head. *Your suffering is never more than your glory that is yours.*

I immediately knew what this meant in spite of its awkward wording. To hear a phrase and instantly understand its meaning is as if God bypasses your own brain synapses so that cerebral processing becomes pointless. He jumps you ahead beyond Scripture 101 and places His message directly into your heart…and you automatically understand. The breadth and depth of His word may not fully manifest within your mind or its application to your own life, but the message is sealed and alive. On this particular night, I still wasn't prepared to associate those words He whispered to me with my own life. I was still blind to that.

While I didn't apply it to myself personally at that time, I associated it with an acupuncture patient of mine who was having immeasurable suffering around her inability to get pregnant. I could identify with her pain even though I already had my two daughters. My daughters were nine and four then, but the agony I endured during my first marriage in my attempt to convince my husband to allow me to come off my birth control was still palpable. I knew the pain my patient suffered when she looked at another pregnant woman or attended a baby shower. I knew what being consumed with this one all-encompassing urge was like. It was unforgiving in its relentless hormonal and emotional pressure.

I used my suffering patient to understand His meaning. I understood the phrase to mean that the suffering she was going through would ultimately pale in comparison to her future happiness. There was a vague awareness that joy and happiness had an otherworldly reality to it. That was all, but it rocked my world at the time because I felt how profound the words were. The cerebral association I had was encouraging and promising, but simple and limited. The far-reaching impact of the phrase didn't reveal itself to me until a few years later in 2005.

✦✦✦✦✦

In 2005, about four years prior to my coming to Christ, I was sitting in the living room. Larry owned a huge King James Bible. A family member had given it to him, but it sat on our bookshelf in the living room as a bookend for other smaller books. For reasons I don't recall, I decided to look through it one evening. It was a very large and beautiful leather-bound heavy Bible. I placed it on my lap. I opened it randomly and began reading. Romans 8:18 is the first phrase I saw.

> *For I reckon that the sufferings of this present time*
> *are not worthy to be compared with the glory*
> *which shall be revealed to us.*
> **Romans 8:18 (KJV)**

It was like a flash of lightning! I felt like a child spilling over with delight on Christmas morning, tearing off the wrapping to the ultimate gift. It mirrored the joy I felt at becoming pregnant on our first try with my daughters! It was like a wave so powerful it would knock me over. The words were there! This is what He had whispered to me in bed that night the years before.

What I realized for the first time was that the God of the universe was talking to me! Romans 8:18 has become a very personal and palpable reminder that Jesus was beckoning and whispering into my life years before I finally gave him my heart. It felt supernatural. It felt metaphysical. But more than anything, it was humbling, because I couldn't understand why He'd even bother with me. So unworthy and irrelevant I was in the scheme of things.

What was it that God was revealing to me personally from Romans 8:18? Being a born again Christian now, since 2009, I feel that I have lived that verse. The joy I have come to know from the faith I have in God and in the hope I have for life, has given me a peace I was incapable of surmising with my own mind. God is teaching me how to love better and live better. He has guided me away from familial conflict and towards reconciliation and healing. Most importantly is

He is teaching me how to love with all of my heart. My faith and hope for my future in His Kingdom after I no longer walk this earth offers me peace even when I face darkened days.

As I record this life-altering incident, I can't help but reflect on the fact that we all have our unique journey in life. How many of us travel through our lives seeking something we can't really define? We all have a story. It's that story that defines us and our identity. It weaves itself into a unique tapestry that becomes the fabric of our lives. It etches itself into our souls. We sojourn on with gusto or with fragile uncertainty and everything in between. We convince ourselves that it is our story and our own will that gets us through. That is our first great self-deception. We begin to think it is our life, and our choices, and our accomplishments, and failures alone that have created our fabric. Our pride takes hold and becomes the blueprint of what we call *self*.

Through it all, we become blind to the unrequited Lover who is only a breath away from our heart. We ignore His presence and misinterpret His whisperings. But Jesus is unrelenting.

By finally accepting Jesus as my personal Savior in September 2009, I unlocked the door to allow full entry. I took His outstretched hand and grabbed hold for dear life. Being reborn began an unfolding of awareness that was both ancient and primal and current simultaneously. I could start to understand with my soul why He loved me. I could slowly meld into His promise and his love. My intellectualized understanding of His love for me became replaced with an embodied joy that could only be about His love.

However, this transformation came very slowly. The process was a relentless, continual pursuit on His part and a gradually increasing surrender on my part. Surrendering my attachment to my interpretation of myself and my place in life was no easy task. The desire and need to interpret my life with my own meager brain was woven so deeply into my being that even as I'd be standing before the King I'd be plagued with "yes, buts…"

CHAPTER 12

An Angel Messenger

*I will instruct you and teach you in the way
you should go. I will counsel you with
my loving eye on you.*
Psalm 32:8 (NIV)

It was the spring of 2003, and I was running late to pick up my daughters from school. Running late was my life. I could blame my lateness on everything and anyone but me, and I used every excuse in the book. I was navigating the challenges of single parenthood while fighting an ugly divorce process alone. Traffic was too congested. I was starting my acupuncture practice, and my patient took too long to get out the door. I had to answer the phone call before I walked out the door. I had to clean out the kitty litter box that was way overdue. I was my mother's daughter and had suffered too many school days waiting for her to kiss her lover goodbye before she would pick me up at the school parking lot curb.

My mother's legacy coursed its breathless, tight-chested anxiety through my body so that this urgency felt like oxygen to my constricted lungs. It was all I knew. The anxious, short-winded in-and-out was my modus operandi.

There I was, rushing down the boulevard, which was about a mile from my daughters' school, when suddenly I saw a flashing light behind me. The binding around my chest became tighter as I pulled my car over to the curb and watched the officer dismount his motorcycle. I began reflecting on the collection of all the speeding moments and rearview gazes at policemen approaching my car. These were my pedal to the metal days, and never had there been a motorcycle! They had always been patrol cars. And never did the officer have those pants that belled out mid-leg. It was like something out of a cartoon. He strode over to my car. We went through the usual exchange of words and documents. I waited while he did his due diligence, cursing quietly under my breath.

I felt the usual sense of guilt that meandered through my brain. In those days, the sense of guilt and *badness* was always a hair's breadth away from every view of a patrol car in my rearview mirror. Even if I wasn't speeding, I'd feel a guilty ping on my soul. If a policeman pulled me over, the sense of guilt weighed on my trembling hand as I offered up my license for inspection.

In those speeding days when I'd rush past a car that felt like it was moving as slowly as a pedaling bike, the driver shooting me a glare or worse, that pang of *badness* and acknowledgment of their judgment would settle over me. They were sealing the stamp of shame. Shame was my shadow and my heart. It followed me everywhere.

An eternity passed as I sat there. The digital clock on my Volvo was banging the passing minutes in my ears, as my daughters gazed up the street looking for my car, or so I imagined. The patrolman returned. I rolled down my window to take the ticket and was face-to-face with his waist and harnessed weapon. His pants were tan, as was his shirt. It was all in slow motion.

Then it happened. He did something that had never been done before. It was as if I was nudged into an altered state beyond my well-practiced ritual of receiving my speeding ticket so I could be on my way. He leaned over and peered into my car, making eye contact with me. I was stunned. My heart became my eyes for the first time in my life. I know this sounds bizarre. However, all I can say is that our mere mortal minds cannot comprehend the idea of seeing with the heart. This is the only way I can describe the moment. I heard him with my heart, as well.

The gatekeeper opens the gate for him, and the sheep recognize his voice and come to him. He calls his own sheep by name and leads them out. After he has gathered his own flock, he walks ahead of them, and they follow him because they know his voice.
John 10:3-4 (NLT)

His voice enveloped me; his gentle concern substantive and consuming. It was as if it wrapped itself around me in a down quilt. It had the depth of an ocean, yet the whisper of dawn. The sound of his voice caught me like a starving fish on a hook, except it was painless and felt like I was aching to be pulled into his net. He leaned over. I saw his face. He looked to be in his thirties, a handsome man. His face was exquisite as his eyes met mine.

That was the moment that my heart became my eyes. To say that he had blue eyes does not begin to do them justice. They drew me in so that nothing else existed at that moment but the shade of blue. I'd been to the Mediterranean in Greece when I was twenty-four years old. His eyes brought that memory back to mind, yet they were more magnificent. His eyes were a shade of blue-green that I'd never seen before.

It was as if his eyes spoke at that moment, and my heart heard the words and my soul listened as he said, "Please, don't speed. Somebody is going to get hurt." That's all he said, yet it was one of those God-stopping moments of my life.

I pray that the eyes of your heart may be enlightened in order that you may know the hope to which he has called you, the riches of his glorious inheritance in his holy people...
Ephesians 1:18 (NIV)

The depth of concern that I *heard* with my heart at that moment was delivered into my tumultuous world like an ocean swelling onto a beach. It was God's ocean. It was His love, His warning, His pleading to me to pull myself together because it was only with my God-given will that I could do so. This was one of my first experiences of hearing God's conviction and receiving it as He intends, with love and without guilt or shame. God's conviction is His way of guiding and correcting us. Because He is Love, His convictions never hurt; they only heal.

The officer then broke the spell and said, "There have been a lot of complaints on Roland Avenue, so we are going to be here for a couple of weeks. Be careful not to get another ticket." When he said this to me, the life-altering moment ceased, and I heard his warning with my ears. My mind went into gear, and I thought about slowing down on my usual route to avoid another ticket.

I will say that I kept a lookout for the next two weeks on that boulevard during the same hours, but I only saw another officer once. Maybe it was another angel interceding for another suffering soul like me. I never saw my angel again, as I had come to think of him. The paper ticket was real. My lateness in picking up my daughters was real. But my stunning moment when God's love mingled inside my heart and soul, quickening a desire for Him, even before I consciously realized that desire, seared itself into my soul.

REJUVENATION

In His river of Grace
Immersed.
Through faith, we endure the raging current.
We hold our stance as the tempest rolls.
Gentle ripples…barely perceptible,
He chips away at our stony selves.
Jesus is relentless in His love and determination
to shape us into His perfect art.
Over and over again,
Deep calls to deep,
the water washes over us as we emerge into His likeness.
He sees what He sees!
He knows what we are and how we will ultimately look.
He sees our beauty when we can't.
He knows every nuance and curve of our face and our body.
Every tear is washed away in the current of His tender love.
Our shell of humanity slowly erodes into His masterpiece.
Like the perfect marble David.
Like the uncut diamond piercing and radiant.
That is our destiny.
And the river rolls on and on and on.

CHAPTER 13

A Parting Gift

So, don't be misled, my dear brothers and
sisters. Whatever is good and perfect is a gift coming down
to us from God our Father, who created all the lights in
the heavens. He never changes or casts a shifting shadow.
He chose to give birth to us by giving us his true word. And
we, out of all creation, became his prized possession.
James 1: 16-18 (NLT)

Looking back, I have no doubt that Jesus brought Kara into my life in the spring of 2004. I was a newly licensed acupuncturist and I met a businesswoman at an event in Baltimore County. After a brief chat, she asked me for my business card so she could make an appointment for acupuncture. Kara was among the group of my first patients I had procured in an effort to build my new clinical practice.

Kara came to acupuncture treatment to address some chronic shooting low back pain she'd had for a few years. We had a great rapport and developed a lovely bond that is one of the benefits of the acupuncture treatment journey. She was planning a move to North Carolina that summer and was seeking work in the Christian ministry. Her goal held no meaning for me because at that point in time, I had no interest in Christianity. Kara would often say that she was *born again* and wanted to *disciple*. I had no clue what she was talking about, and she didn't elaborate, nor did I ask. To this day, I don't know if her not explaining herself was her approach to discipling, or she was too new at her mission to know how to deal with a non-believer like myself.

At this point in my life, I was an *all roads lead to God* kind of gal. I had completed the rigors of acupuncture school and the self-reflection process that demands. I was *Zen*, as people would put it. And I was Jewish. As a Jew, I believed that even speaking the name *Jesus* was taboo. I'm sure that part of my resistance to learning more about Kara's "born again" status was due to this visceral belief that Jesus was off-limits for me.

My parents put my siblings and me through a few years of Sunday school at our synagogue Har Sinai. While we uniformly hated Sunday school, we dutifully endured the four hours on Sunday mornings, fighting to stay awake in class. We tried to memorize the Hebrew alphabet and learn some Hebrew psalms. We attempted to memorize the required Jewish holidays and their meanings. I don't think I'm speaking just for myself when I say the boredom was deadening.

For me, the light at the end of this weekly tunnel was the arrival back home and the lunch my father had prepared for us. To this day, I can still taste the milkshake and egg salad sandwich with lettuce and tomatoes on lightly toasted bread that he lovingly prepared for us ahead of time.

While I hated Sunday school, I do not remember ever lacking a sense of awe when I entered the sanctuary at Har Sinai. Sometimes when going from one class to another on a Sunday school morning, I'd open the door to the sanctuary and go sit in one of the cushioned chairs to simply be in that space. I knew it was His space. Har Sinai had a beautiful golden dome on the outside. From the inside, I would daydream, staring up at its domed vault with the recessed lights randomly placed in its ceiling. He was there. I knew it, I felt it, and I longed for it. I experienced a *knowing* about God as a child that was everpresent.

Har Sinai was a Reform congregation. Reformed Judaism, for me, was the most washed down and secularized form of our religion. It was liturgical and ritualistic. While they incorporated Hebrew into the worship service, the experience was shallow and unfulfilling. At a core level, I knew it was empty. On a visceral level, I felt the lack of sincere, heartfelt worship or awe for our Creator. As a young Jewish girl, I felt it on a level that was reflective of my limited understanding of what worshipping God meant. When in synagogue during the High Holy Days, I still recall my mother and aunt talking quietly in the row behind me, and I knew it was disrespectful and it disappointed me.

I look back now in utter gratitude that I was blessed with the appetite to seek Him. I was fortunate to have a subtle but gnawing hunger for Him, and at the same time a dissatisfaction and even a vague sense of shame at the disregard that my Jewish family had for Him. On some deep and yet unformed level, I knew that we were missing the mark in honoring God.

While I don't recall ever being taught that Jesus was anathema to Jews, I do know that the message was subliminally communicated. Whether it was an archetypal legacy that transferred through our DNA or silent whisperings of the collective Jewish soul, Jesus was not to be discussed. His name was not to be uttered. To even speak His name felt like blasphemy.

In 2004 when Kara came to my acupuncture treatment room for her last session before she moved to North Carolina, she handed me a CD as a parting gift. She apologized for the lack of original packaging, as it had been lost somewhere in her toddler's bedroom. This was the CD she'd have him listen to during naptime and bedtime. As it turns out, this became my first exposure to contemporary worship music.

One day in the late summer of 2004, I listened to it for the first time in my car. It remained in my CD player permanently that year. I instantly loved the music and the lyrics. Like a starving person who feasts ravenously on their first meal, I listened to it continuously and solely until I ventured into deeper waters later that year. I still have that CD a decade later, without its packaging, but I don't play it anymore because it has too many scratches. With both a sense of guilt and exhilarating defiance, I tuned in to a new local Christian radio station (95.1 SHINE-FM) in early 2006. It remains my station to this day.

My car became my sanctuary. In a state of denial, I was tiptoeing into deeper waters. Looking back on what I refer to as my closet Christian days, I smile to myself as I ponder Jesus' sweet joy as he gazed at this lost Jewish woman wandering slowly in His direction.

CHAPTER 14

Avalon

*Sing a new song to the Lord! Let the whole earth sing
to the Lord! Sing to the Lord; praise his name.
Each day proclaim the good news that he saves.*
Psalm 96: 1-2 (NLT)

I discovered the joyful inspiration of the band Avalon's music in 2004 during my early years as a self-declared *closet Christian*. The CD that had been given to me had a number of their songs on it. I played their music so frequently that my car became my sanctuary. I only listened to contemporary Christian worship songs when I was alone in my car or my young daughters were with me. The music was uplifting and had a great beat. I'd have danced in the car if I could have.

When I heard Avalon was coming to my hometown in concert, I had to go. This was a huge decision because I hadn't admitted to anyone that my heart was being tugged in Christ's direction. I hadn't even admitted it to myself. Finding someone to go with me proved a challenge. Going alone just was not an option at that point in time. I had a sense of guilt, fear, and profound disloyalty to my Jewish heritage. Going with a friend would have helped mute that somewhat. In the end, I found a neighbor to join me.

It was Friday night at a mega-church in Baltimore County. This was my first time entering a church on my own accord, instead of an invitation to someone's wedding or Christmas mass or a funeral.

This action was self-initiated. I bought two tickets, for me and a friend, and we went.

It struck me at how un-church-like this place looked. It was modern and massive. There was no crucifix or stained glass anywhere. If I didn't know it was a church, I would have assumed it was a theater. It was a packed house, with nearly four thousand seats.

Once the lights dimmed, and the music started, I was struck by a sensation in my chest. It was either a tightening or an expansiveness that felt like my heart was pressing all the space within my ribcage. "Testify" was their first song, and I stood up with half the audience. I was a bit embarrassed at my reaction, but I simply could not remain seated. While I was not a hand raiser yet, as that would come years later, I stood in awe as I allowed myself to feel the magnitude of being surrounded by other human beings who loved the Lord. It took my breath away, and I began to cry. I cried through most of the performance. The welling up of emotions could only be described as coming home after a lifetime of being gone. It was an experience of the heart and the spirit. There were no thoughts. There was only a flood of emotions.

Coming to this event was like a release of something for me. I'm not sure if it was bondage loosening or me exhaling after spending my life in a breath-holding pattern. I felt absolute knee-dropping gratitude for finally experiencing what I always knew was missing during my childhood synagogue days. This was what it was like to worship in the presence of God. To be, for the first time, in a room full of people who were all celebrating God was one of the most exhilarating moments of my life!

I was overwhelmed by all of it, and it took my breath away. I glanced down at my friend who came with me. She was seated, but I could see out of the corner of my eye that she was watching me cry. At the time, I was embarrassed. I didn't understand it. It was something I simply could not control or contain. This was bigger than me. It was larger than my embarrassment.

I understand now that it was the Holy Spirit moving within

me. It was the Holy Spirit waking me up. It was the Holy Spirit welcoming me home. My heart was wide open. I didn't understand it. This baby pre-Christian was swept away that night. Joy whisked me away as it spilled over and over in waves of tears and a swelling heart.

Let the heavens be glad, and the earth rejoice!
Let the sea and everything in it shout his praise!
Let the fields and their crops burst out with joy!
Let the trees of the forest sing for joy!
Psalm 96: 11-12 (NLT)

CHAPTER 15

Phoenix Rising

*My heart pounds in my chest. The terror of death
assaults me. Fear and trembling overwhelm me,
and I can't stop shaking. Oh, that I had wings like
a dove; then I would fly away and rest! I would
fly far away to the quiet of the wilderness.*
Psalm 55:4-7 (NLT)

The spring of 2006 was a knee-dropping season for me. My
mother had taken ill and had her first serious hospitalization at
Greater Baltimore Medical Center. My brother, sister, and I realized
that this could have been the end for her. These were a trying several
weeks of her being dehydrated, with an infection that left her weak
and hallucinating.

Since my brother lived in New Jersey, my sister and I tag-teamed
visits to the hospital to support Mom. We were like a well-oiled
machine. The history of contention between us had dissolved as we
banded together to support our mother.

Little did we know that once she was stable enough to be
transferred to a rehab nursing facility, she would endure several
more hospitalizations for the same issues until her death in 2012.
My sister and I continued to effectively tag team supportive visits to
the nursing facility; she from her home five minutes away, me from
my home half an hour away.

I was also a few weeks past my fourth and final court experience in Annapolis, Maryland, to deal with custody and financial issues with my former husband. I was trying to secure and build my acupuncture practice, which at the time was split between two locations in different parts of Baltimore County. I was adapting to being remarried. My daughters were ten and fourteen years old. I was driving them from our home in the county to their private school in the city forty minutes away. I felt like I was living in my car in between acupuncture patients and highway commutes and a sick mother.

To say that my life was bursting at the seams with demands both energetically and emotionally is a monumental understatement. In retrospect, all of this would have been a piece of cake if not for the shattering event that occurred on March 29, 2006. As some Star Wars fans would say, there had been *a disturbance in the force.*

My sister's son had been found dead in his New York City apartment. My brilliant, creative twenty-six-year-old nephew was gone. He had vanished from the orbit of our lives. My sister went *missing in action* as well. Her heart had shattered, and she recoiled into her house in pain, shock, and numbness. Her visits to our mother ceased immediately.

Throughout our lives, my mother always seemed threatened when my sister and I reconnected and behaved as best friends. As young teens, she'd hover when my sister and I had alone time chatting in our bedroom. She'd often speak behind the back of one or the other, seeding discord between the two of us. Ironically, when she was hospitalized, my sister, and I instantly reconciled. By the grace of God, this was the state of our relationship when my nephew died.

As a result of my nephew's death, the vigil my sister and I shared became my singular burden overnight. I went from sitting vigil for one person to doing so for two. My sister was now front and center in my heart and mind. Despite the off and on contentiousness between my sister and me, she was my soulmate. She was my priority. My nephew's death put a spotlight on the magnitude of importance that my sister had in my life.

When I received the news over the phone from my sister's neighbor I began screaming. My terrified daughters came running into my room. I kept sobbing and screaming my sister's name repeatedly. My daughters pleaded with me to answer them. It terrified them that their aunt might have been in an accident or died. I could only cry and repeat over and over again, "What am I going to do about my sister?" It was as if the tragedy had happened to me. My sister's pain became mine.

What do you do with the person whose soul is intertwined with yours? I recall driving home one afternoon that April after my nephew's death and spotted two dogwood trees blooming, one pink and one white. They were planted so close to each other that they had become entwined so that the two trees looked like one with two colors. It was a stunning sight. The imagery of the trees struck me with a familiarity that whispered from my heart. It reminded me of my relationship with my sister. I remember thinking, *What if one of them dies? What would happen to the other?*

The first night of this tragedy, the family gathered. My brother and his family drove down from New Jersey. I canceled all work, left my husband Larry to watch over my daughters, and I went to be at my sister's side. I slept there for a few nights. The first night I slept with my sister in her king-sized bed. My sister lay in those darkened hours between her daughter and me. I didn't sleep that first night. I laid there with my hand over my sister's heart, literally on her chest. In my helpless state, I felt that by leaving my hand over her heart, I could keep it from ceasing to beat. Or if it did stop beating, I'd be ready to save her life. She felt like a fragile bird underneath my own vigilant palm.

My sister was one of those strikingly beautiful women who commanded the space she occupied. She personified the firstborn of the sibling order. Her son's death left her withering in slow motion before my eyes. With her larger-than-life presence, I had spent my life up to this point feeling like I lived in her shadow. However, I'd have rather endured that than watch her lose her brilliance. She was like an exquisite diamond that I couldn't allow to go dull. We were that magnificent pink and white dogwood, and I couldn't allow it to wither.

As a result, I spent the next twelve months on call for her. There were frequent visits to just be with her. There were her unpredictable phone calls. No matter where I was or who I was with, even if I were with a patient, if my caller ID displayed her number, I'd answer. Most poignant were the middle-of-the-night breathy, barely audible telephone calls from her. In those silent lonely hours, all she wanted to do was die. I had not come to Christ yet, so all I had to give was my simple sisterly love and listening. My fear of losing her kept me vigilant, alert, and ready. All I could do was hold the space for her shrinking heart. It felt like I was breathing for her in those silent hours of the night.

I was so focused on her welfare, all the while continuing to visit my mother and deal with the rehab facility's discharge planning, that I never realized or released my own grief over losing my nephew. That finally began to happen nearly a year later during an acupuncture treatment I was receiving. I had developed a chronic ache in my right shoulder and clavicle. My acupuncturist and I discussed its location near the heart and lung. We understood from an Eastern Medical perspective that it was an energetic cul-de-sac for grief. As we explored further I recalled that it all began that spring of 2006. My acupuncturist sat with me as my convulsive tears began to finally release over the loss of my nephew.

With these events as a backdrop, I was driving on the expressway one afternoon in April 2006. I had seen a few patients in my Towson office and then had visited my mother at the facility. I was rushing downtown to pick up my daughters from school, trying to figure out how I was going to get home in time to make dinner and then go back to be with my sister. At this time, I did not yet know Jesus, but I was beginning to listen to worship music. I was starting to hear Him whisper to me through the lyrics of the songs. I was blind to the magnitude of what was happening to me in relation to Him, but at least I was following His lead, albeit blindly. I have a vague recollection of myself driving down that expressway and crying and appealing to God to give me something to help me. What I remember is how deeply sorry for myself I felt. I hated my life and saw no end to the sadness. In that moment, I didn't even know what to ask for. But I silently and wordlessly prayed as I drove downtown.

Then, like the Phoenix that rose from the ashes, I experienced what I recall as a slow-motion miracle. It occurred in a matter of fifteen to twenty seconds.

The lead foot I had as a driver at the time was weighing heavy on the gas pedal as I rushed down that expressway. I was in the middle lane when far off to the right, high above some trees, perhaps a mile away, something caught my eye. It looked like pieces of litter being tossed about in the space above the trees.

I watched one white piece of crumpled paper separate from the others and pass in front of my car about a hundred yards away and gently land in the fast lane to my left. Upon landing, I was shocked to see that it was not paper, but a white dove! I was horrified when a car immediately sped past me in the fast lane and drove right over it. I expected to see feathers and blood with roadkill left in its path, but instead the bird was immaculately intact as it lifted off, flying away, a safe distance from my windshield.

At the time I knew that something miraculous had occurred. It was too surreal to believe that a bird would survive a car driving over it at that speed. The wind tunnel from the car should have tossed it violently into the wheels or underbody of the car. When I'd recount the story to others, I'd wonder if I had imagined the whole thing.

It wasn't until a few years later after coming to Christ that I fully began to understand and appreciate what had occurred. Whether it was a divine vision or a miracle, I know that Jesus was revealing Himself to me on that highway and stepping into my tortured spring of 2006 to love on me. He was showing me He was in my life. He was revealing how even I would rise again in ways I could not yet imagine. It was a foreshadowing of my own rebirth once I accepted Him as my Savior. I would rise from the death of my existence and, in my rebirth, my life would become something I couldn't even fathom in the spring of 2006.

As I look back on my years as a *baby Christian*, I reflect on that event and feel so painfully unworthy of Him even bothering to step into my life at that moment. Looking back on it as a maturing Christian, I marvel at Jesus' sweet, loving patience as He slowly helped me understand how deeply he loved me.

> *I look up to the mountains—does my help come from there?*
> *My help comes from the Lord who made heaven and earth!*
> **Psalm 121: 1-2 (NLT)**

CHAPTER 16

Intercession on 695 South

The Lord himself watches over you!
The Lord stands beside you as your protective shade. The sun will
not harm you by day, nor the moon at night. The Lord keeps
you from all harm and watches over your life. The Lord keeps
watch over you as you come and go, both now and forever.
Psalm 121:5-8 (NLT)

I was driving home from visiting my grieving sister and picking up my daughters from school. My head was spinning with to-do-lists and grief. My nephew was buried the prior week and life as I knew it had entered an unwelcomed new orbit.

Suddenly my cell phone rang. On the other end was a concerned voice. He said, "Jill, this is Medford. Remember me? From the vacuum store?" Medford was a kind elderly gentleman whom I hadn't spoken with in nearly two years.

Two years prior, during my packing process to move to Catonsville, I had frequented a vacuum store in the city where Medford would give me boxes I needed for packing. He was a tall, distinguished African American man about twenty years my senior. I enjoyed chatting with him because his aura of ease in simply being himself was comforting. He was gracious and generous with his kindness. We had a simple relationship that consisted of my brief encounters with him in the shop. I was always rushing in those days, but that never seemed to affect his patience and kindness toward me. The last time we spoke, I gave him my acupuncture business card because he mentioned his wife's hip pain. I also recall him mentioning his Christian bible study group, which meant very little to me at the time.

When I heard his voice at the other end of the phone, I assumed he was calling me on behalf of his wife. This was not the case. Instead, he said, "Jill, I have your business card here on my desk. You've been on my mind for a while now. I decided to just call you…. Jill…is everything all right? Are you okay?"

I nearly cried as I told him about what had transpired with my nephew, and sister and mother. Then Medford said, "Now Jill…you know how you are. You always focus on everyone else's needs but your own. It's very important for you to drink enough water and eat healthy right now. Do not forget to take care of you!" What was so amazing about his comments is that he spoke to me as if we'd known each other for many years. He offered instructions to me that assumed he knew my life patterns. He didn't *know how I was* with people!

Medford was God's angel at that moment. He had decided to heed God's command to intercede on my behalf. Although I was a number of years away from accepting Jesus into my life, God used Medford to let me know that I was being watched over.

I have tucked Medford's telephone call into a sweet memory vault in my mind because of what he did for me. Medford reached out and loved on me. He was obedient to the Lord's command to do His work.

God is like that; He sends nutritious little breadcrumbs along the path to Jesus like Manna from Heaven. I wonder how many other sweet moments there were that I had missed along the way because of the chaos and busyness in my life.

When you go through deep waters I will be with you. When
you go through rivers of difficulty you will not drown.
Isaiah 43:2 (NLT)

CHAPTER 17

She's Not My Mother Anymore!

*But the time is coming—indeed it's here now—
when true worshippers will worship the Father in spirit
and in truth. The Father is looking for those who will
worship him that way. For God is Spirit, so those who
worship him must worship in spirit and in truth.*
John 4:23-24 (NLT)

My heart raged over the news I had just received. I was standing in the parking lot of Charlestown Church. It was a beautiful summer day in 2006 as I stood outside, but inside, my heart was stormy.

I kept myself available to my sister nonstop since her son died in March 2006. I was attending a funeral one afternoon for the deceased father of a friend when my caller ID displayed my sister's number. When I saw her number, I excused myself to answer. She was extremely agitated. I could barely make out her words. This was not unusual as of late, as she journeyed through the murky waters of a grieving mother. She had been thrust into the membership of a club I wanted nothing to do with—ever. However, as her sister, my promise was to never let go of her. I would not allow her to drown in her grief.

She began to relate to me what had occurred a few hours prior.

She had ventured out to visit our bedridden mother for the first time since her son had died. This was a feat in itself, due to the nature of their relationship, because my sister had traveled the same path with my mother as I had. This adulterous path was our shared journey.

She was in my mother's bedroom and had brought her two little dogs, Willy and Franky, with her. Being tiny terriers, she let them wander the bedroom with their leashes attached.

At that time, my mother had another visitor. Jesse, the final man in her life, was there tending to her. My sister had an amicable relationship with Jesse, while I mostly kept my distance.

As she chatted with him and my mother, Franky and Willy got their leashes tangled around the legs of our mother's walker. As the walker magically began to move on its own with the dogs wandering about, my mother's cat, which had been perched on the high dresser, jumped down to attack. I always called this cat the *hellcat* because it was so unfriendly and sinister. The cat attacked my sister's bare legs. With my sister terrorized and screaming, Jesse was able to pull him off of her.

This news horrified me. After hearing my sister's account of her visit to the doctor, I asked what our mother said when this happened. She informed me that our mother's response was, "Why doesn't anyone get upset when I bleed?" Those self-absorbed words were the final blow to my tenuous bond with my mother.

I looked up at the sky and declared with all of my heart, "She is no longer my mother, and I am no longer her daughter!" In my mind and soul, I had finally *divorced* her. I didn't know at that moment what that would look like, but I knew that a major shift had decisively happened for me in relation to my mother. At this time, I was not yet a Christian. I was sticking my toe into the waters of this relationship with Jesus, but I had three years to go before I'd settle into His arms. As the words I had just declared in my heart began to take shape in my mind, I was aware of a message that suddenly planted itself there as well. The words were: "your job is to save your mother spiritually." Later, I would understand this experience as the

Holy Spirit's conviction. I know looking back that He was present at that moment with me. He placed His words into my mind and heart with a decisive conviction.

While I knew that being her daughter in the flesh created only pain and empty space, what filled it was the mission that was suddenly planted in my heart. I did not understand what *saving* my mother would *look like.* But this command that the Holy Spirit placed in my heart allowed me to continue in a relationship with her. It allowed me to be supportive. It allowed me to visit her and chat on the phone; all the activities that a daughter would do with a bedbound mother.

Participating in this *spiritual saving* would manifest itself several years later in October 2009, one month after I came to Christ. It was a life-altering incident in my living room between me and my mother and my pastor. What I marvel at now, looking back, is that God will guide us and shepherd us even if we are not yet Christ-followers. In partnership with Jesus, the work God sets out for us to accomplish for Him becomes empowered by His hand, even before we recognize it.

> *I have told you all this so that you may have peace in me.*
> *Here on earth you will have many trials and sorrows.*
> *But take heart, because I have overcome the world.*
> **John 16:33 (NLT)**

CONFESSION

You beckoned me from before time.
I gazed up...my eyes drawn toward Your love.
You towered over my home, my town.
In Your patient gaze, I wandered
meandering, disconnected paths
tangled and lost,
thorns and confusion.
And then there You were...
You wrapped Your Love around me.
Like a breath,
next a touch...
as light as a feather.
I was swaddled by love.
"How could You love me?"
My unworthiness...your treasure?
Why would You love me?
And then again, there You were!
A streak of white across my path,
As I raced down the highway of my life...
my life...my anguish.
My sorrow...my pain.
You touched my heart from without.... From within.
All the while knowing my first love...my sin.
You guided me here.... Blessings undeserved.
My sanctuary on Patleigh.

The silent deer…only Mackenzie can hear
The prayers from Your children.
My oasis…undeserved.
Your patience…unrelenting.
My breath nearly gone.
My life laid to waste.
Your Holy Love was planted within.
I drop to my knees
and hand You my sin.

CHAPTER 18

The Eye of God

*For I hold you by your right hand—I, the Lord your
God. And I say to you, "Don't be afraid. I am here to
help you. Though you are a lowly worm, O Jacob,
don't be afraid, people of Israel, for I will help you.
I am the Lord, your Redeemer.
I am the Holy One of Israel."*
Isaiah 41:13-14 (NLT)

The spring of 2006 began the unfolding of the days of my
deliverance. Unbeknownst to me, I was in the process of
finding my way into Jesus' pasture. In the tumult and chaos and
white-knuckled days of my ongoing divorcing legal process from my
first husband, God was allowing me to play out my own drama as I
slowly dismantled my former life. While I was too in the thick of it
to realize it at the time, I would come out on the other side reborn.

This was the spring of what would turn out to be my last go-
around with the court system regarding my divorce. My former
husband had appealed the previous court decision, which had granted
me full custody and retention of child support for my daughters.

I could no longer afford my attorney. My debt from the divorce
process along with my acupuncture school loan had taken a financial
toll. By the grace of God, a close friend of my sister's offered to help
prepare me to appear before the Court of Appeals in Annapolis,
Maryland. Because she was a lawyer, she could take me to the law

library at the University of Maryland and teach me to sort through previous cases to support my argument that it was in my daughters' best interest to remain in my full custody.

The weekend before the court case, I had to go to the print shop to duplicate documents I needed for court the following Tuesday morning. As I walked into the shop that Saturday morning, life felt surreal in my disconnected state of mind. All I had in my consciousness were the legal arguments that my law coach Cindy and I had been reciting over and over. Nothing else mattered. My appetite had vanished. My emotional state hovered somewhere between depressed and numb. Staving off daily panic attacks was the best I could do leading up to my court date. My role as mother to my daughters had deteriorated into simply going through the motions. Life felt like I was going through it a day at a time at best, or an hour at a time at worst. The fear of losing child support and custody was a dark cloud that permeated everything like an emotional thick fog.

This particular print shop had four copy machines. I walked over to the one that was free and lifted the flap so I could place my first paper on the smooth glass surface. There was something on the glass that someone had left behind. It was a thin green cardboard insert to a cassette tape. What stood out to me was the immediate awareness that this was not an accident. I knew instinctively that it was left there for me. There were only two words written on the side facing up: "Black Gospel."

At this point, I had been dabbling in Christian music, which stirred up more seeking and questioning about who Jesus was. My car had become my private sanctuary. I was not a self-declared *closet Christian* yet, but looking back, my heart was beginning to slowly open to His whisperings. When I saw the title, I had no doubt it was for me. I turned over the insert to see what had been copied by its previous owner. I stood there in awe and read through the lyrics. What follows is the title and some of the lyrics.

"I WON'T LET GO"

There is no trial that He can't bring me through
There is no tunnel that He can't bring light to

Trials worketh patience, and patience worketh hope
In spite of my situation, I won't let go.
There is no problem I know that God can't solve
When I got into it He was already involved

REPEAT CHORUS:

You may be weary and feel you can't go on
My friend take courage, in Christ you must be strong

(author unknown)

When God steps into your life with such a simultaneously bold and subtle action, all you can do is kneel before the King. I obviously didn't physically kneel in the middle of the print store. At that point in my life I was still a lost and wandering Jew. I really didn't know Jesus yet. I was simply a fractured woman who was confused and overwhelmed. There was nothing about me at that moment in time that felt particularly loveable or worthy of Him taking the time to directly step into my messy life, yet He did. I knew it and reread the lyrics in amazement.

What happened next was equally impacting. A black van pulled up to the outside of the shop along the curb. This was noticeable because the driver didn't park in the lot; she pulled up to the curb with her flashers on. The driver was obviously making a quick stop. Once again, I knew who she was. I knew the driver was the owner of this insert. I knew she was coming back for it. How did I know? When it's a *God thing*, you just know.

An African American woman stepped out and walked into the store with a searching look in her gaze. She turned toward me, and I held the insert up to her. I asked if it was hers, and she acknowledged that it was. She said she was copying the lyrics for her church the next morning. I asked if I could make a copy for myself. She smiled and said, "Yes, of course!"

For the second time in two years, I saw the eyes. Unlike the brilliant blue of the police officer on Roland Avenue two years before, her eyes were striking shades of rosy fuchsia. The color itself is actually indescribable, but the experience was identical to my previous encounter with the policeman. I can only describe it as having seen the color of her eyes with my heart. It was as if all I could see were her eyes and their exquisite color. I can see them even now as I write this passage over a decade later. Her eyes were all-consuming. For that moment in time, I was lost inside of the image of them.

I copied the lyrics and handed the insert back to her. She smiled and left. To anyone watching us, it appeared to be a momentary, cordial interaction between two women. But for me at that moment, the Earth moved. God was present, and only I knew it. Maybe she knew too. Perhaps she was an angel sent by Him, or a Christian being obedient to the call and interceding on my behalf. Maybe not. All I know is that God stepped in at that moment to breathe His life-giving love and strength into my fragile self. I keep a laminated copy of the insert in my wallet, and I tape it to my weekly calendar to this day.

------------ ✦✦✦✦✦✦ ------------

The court case in Annapolis, Maryland, ended up being the final judicial experience between my former husband and myself. He sat at the table beside me with his lawyer, and I sat alone without representation. My *coach* Cindy sat in the audience beside my husband, Larry. I was allowed to go first and was given ten minutes to make my case. When the green light illuminated for me to stand up and start speaking, I froze. I lost nearly twenty seconds of my allotted time trying to gather my capacity to utter a sound. I had struggled with severe panic attacks for the last three decades and was afraid I'd have another as I stood in front of the courtroom. I can only say that by the grace of God, once I finally began to speak, the words flowed out of my mouth so clearly, firmly, and precisely, that when the red light illuminated, you could hear a pin drop in the courtroom. My former husband's lawyer's head was literally resting on her arm at her table. It was if she wilted over the ten minutes that I spoke, or the Holy Spirit spoke through me. She knew that her case was defeated even before she had a chance to stand and respond.

People gazed at me as I made my way back to my seat beside Larry and Cindy. Afterward, people asked me if I was a lawyer. People approached Cindy to see if she would coach them as well. Needless to say, I won that case. I retained sole custody of my daughters and my child support, and my former husband was even required to pay all court costs.

Don't be afraid, for I am with you. Don't be discouraged,
for I am your God. I will strengthen you and help you. I
will hold you up with my victorious right hand. "See, all
your angry enemies lie there, confused and humiliated.
Anyone who opposes you will die and come to nothing.
Isaiah 41: 10-11 (NLT)

———————— ✦✦✦✦✦ ————————

Three years later in 2009, I was taking an introductory class at my church for new Christians called Starting Point. Several sessions into the class, a gentleman brought in a photograph of one of the Hubble telescope pictures from space. It was called the "Eye of God." I had never seen the photo or even heard about the Eye of God. It took my breath away. "That's what I saw!" I proclaimed to the attendees as I shared the stories about the police officer and the woman in the print shop. The colors and the shape in the photograph of the Eye of God were identical to what I saw with my heart on those two occasions.

It was the first time I shared my story about the experience of seeing a person's eyes with my heart. As Christians who believe in miracles, they all understood. Their acceptance of my story helped me to begin to fully appreciate the patient and persistent shepherding that Jesus was doing in my life.

But the Lord says, "The captives of warriors
will be released, And the plunder of tyrants will be retrieved. For
I will fight those who fight you, and I will save your children.
Isaiah 49:25 (NLT)

CHAPTER 19

The Black Wrap

You prepare a feast for me in the presence of my enemies; You honor me by anointing my head with oil. My cup overflows with blessings. Surely goodness and unfailing love will pursue me all the days of my life, and I will live in the house of the LORD forever.
Psalm 23:5-6 (NLT)

The heat was sweltering outside on a muggy Maryland Sunday morning in June 2009. I was bringing my husband, Larry, with me to introduce him to the church I had begun to attend. I was still a wandering Jew who had not yet accepted Christ as her Savior. Maybe because of my excitement, or maybe because of the heat, I realized as we were walking through the parking lot into Grace Community Church that I'd absentmindedly left my wrap at home. I have always needed something to drape over my shoulders and arms when I'm in air conditioning.

As I walked into the church, the enemy was at play for I was cursing to myself. I didn't want the discomfort of the cold air to distract me from the experience. Worship time was so powerful for me and I reveled in the flood of emotion I felt while singing His praises. Watching everyone stand and sing, some with hands raised or swaying, moved me with delight and joy. I'm glad to say that it has the same effect even now as I record this ten years later.

Larry and I entered the church and there was a crowd of people from the earlier service still lingering in the hallway. That was significant because it set the stage for what happened next. Rather than mingle out in the hall with strangers, I followed Larry into the sanctuary. The sanctuary was nearly empty. Everyone from the first service was out in the hall or in the parking lot going home. Grace Community Church is another one of those mega-type churches without the traditional crucifix or stained glass. The sanctuary looks more like a theater than a church. It probably seats at least a thousand people per service.

Larry took the lead and he found his way to a row that was practically dead center in the sanctuary. I went around him and sat to his left. As I sat down, I noticed something draped over the back of the space beside me. It was a neatly folded black cashmere wrap. Someone had left it behind. At first, I did nothing. I sat there in a state of silent, humorous shock. I wanted to put it on, but I felt odd about that. After all, it didn't belong to me. Over the next ten to fifteen minutes, I had a back-and-forth conversation with myself about the inappropriateness of me putting it around my shoulders. I sensed the humor and graciousness of Jesus. As more people filled the auditorium, I knew I had to decide or else my inner dialogue about how cold I was would distract me from the service.

I decided that this was Jesus nodding to me. This was His way of welcoming me into His home. This was His gracious way of loving on and comforting me. I knew that He wouldn't want me cold and distracted from the Word or the opportunity to worship and honor Him.

I put that black wrap around my shoulders and accepted His gift. In my mind, I nodded back to Him as I imagined him smiling down at me. I felt singled out on that particular day. Knowing Jesus treats all of His children in an individual fashion; for me on that day, I felt special and so sweetly loved by Him.

I knew in my heart how delighted He was with me, stepping into His boat from the wild sea of my life. Why He would love me or care so much about me, I still haven't fully grasped. I understand it intellectually, but I still can't fathom it. In moments as I journey on, I know He directly loves me. I can grasp His tender love and protection for me in occasional moments. Maybe He designed us to not absorb it completely until we finally meet Him face to face, because a prolonged or extended period of awe would overwhelm our fragile hearts and minds. He forbade Moses to look upon Him. The curtain of ancient Hebrews kept us separate from His face. Our lives here on earth are the appetizers before the feast He will offer us in His kingdom.

Deep calls to deep
In the roar of your waterfalls;
All your waves and breakers
Have swept over me.
Psalm 42:7 (NIV)

DEEP CALLS TO DEEP

A hardened heart.
Compassion, a shallow pool.
But deep calls to deep.
You did not leave me in that shallow, muddy place.
I saw myself
Going through only the motions of love.
The phony dance of love.
Oh, how I loved to dance.
My mother taught me to dance.
But deep calls to deep,
and You did not forsake me
in that place.
My heart forgotten.
My eyes blinded from You,
Pride set this survival dance.
Self-disdain,
Still deep called to deep.
I begin to see a clearing ahead.
And I begin to remember…
There's light in the distance
And deep calls to deep.

CHAPTER 20

A Wandering Jew Finds Jesus

*The Lord says, "I was ready to respond, but no one
asked for help. I was ready to be found, but no one
was looking for me. I said, 'Here I am, here I am!'
to a nation that did not call on my name."*
Isaiah 65: 1(NLT)

How, might you ask, does a Jewish woman who grew up in a mostly Jewish community wander into the arms of Jesus?

Growing up in a *reformed* Jewish home simply did not provide the religious or spiritual structure I hungered for. Reformed Judaism is what I refer to as the most washed-down version of Judaism you will find. Reform Jews don't keep Kosher. Reform Jews may or may not go to synagogue on the High Holy days such as Rosh Hashana and/or Yom Kippur, and we endure the yearly ritual of reading through the Haggadah on Passover.

For me, the joy over the Passover Seders was only about the aroma from my maternal grandmother's matzo ball soup coming from the kitchen. She was a Russian immigrant, having come to America to escape the pogroms against the Jews in Russia in the 1890s. Her love language was cooking for her family. She retained and shared with us the delectable recipes from her own youth in Russia. One of my prized possessions is her massive tin mixing bowl, which I acquired when my mother died. It looks beat up and dented throughout from the countless chopping episodes where my grandmother would sit at the kitchen table and do her work. It's shallow in depth but about eighteen inches wide with handles. I'd sit and watch her make her dough for sugar cookies using the same recipe for her apple pie crusts. That bowl, like a sacred singing bowl, was where she created her delicious potato blintzes and stuffed knishes.

I recall her chicken broth and how she saved the delectable chicken fat on her kitchen counter for later use in place of butter. She'd use it for the base broth of her Matza ball soup. Grandma's rice puddings, cheese and potato blintzes and hot borscht soup with sour cream were tasty morsels of Jewish memories.

On Passover, or the frequent Sunday family dinners, we'd sit at the ten-foot-long dinner table that was actually a ping-pong table covered with tablecloths. With stomachs growling, we'd wait for Grandma to bring out our meal. But nowhere was God present. During the Seder, we might loosely refer to Him when we would open the door to allow Elijah to enter at his sacred calling into the mystery of the Passover ritual. But beyond that, God remained obscure and simply assumed, as in the high, vaulted dome of my synagogue.

The glory and freedom that is the essence of a personal relationship with God was concealed somewhere in the ethers… or beyond my view where the choir sang on the High Holy days in the synagogue. They sang like angels from afar—never seen, never joyous, and never passionate. If the synagogue *elders'* intent was to create a feeling of God as a mysterious presence, they succeeded. But in that process, it left me empty-handed. It wasn't enough for me.

Maybe it was enough for the congregants in the sanctuary who quietly whispered to each other throughout the services. However, it left me wanting more. My only explanation is that God planted this seed of discontent in me for a reason.

My first husband and I divorced in 2000. We were married for twelve years and blessed with two beautiful little girls. Being thrust into single parenting was a mountain I had no choice but to climb. By the grace of God, I was not in the *single* world very long. Shortly into that journey, I met Larry Smith, a *non-Jew* and a Christian. He was the blue-eyed man who became my cherished second husband.

I smile as I recall the moment I met Larry. To say that his *entry* into my life was a *God thing* is an understatement. I recall his smile before I even met him, as I was driving up the road to pick up my daughters from summer camp in July 1999. I was listening to a song on the radio, "I Knew I Loved You Before I Met You." In my mind's eye I felt the glowing smile of a man. No face. No name. This smile warmed my heart and made me giddy with anticipation. I knew on a visceral level that this was the man I'd eventually meet. The joy I felt as I passed through the intersection of that drive to my children left me brimming with hope.

A few weeks after that, my friend and her husband chaperoned me to a nightclub to go dancing. It was on that night in July that I met the man I now refer to as *my Larry*. We danced, and he gave me that beaming smile that is uniquely his. It was as if time stood still and I was riveted. I knew in that instant that he was who I saw in my mind in the car that sultry afternoon on the highway. As we swayed to the music, and he told me his name, and I realized he wasn't Jewish, I felt an immediate sense of relief. My only explanation for this reaction was that on a deeper level, not yet conscious on my part, I was headed for a new valley. I would leave the Jewish valley I'd dwelled in for my whole life behind, and it delighted me.

My courtship with Larry carried me through my divorce challenges and acupuncture school. My every other weekend time with him would rejuvinate me from the battle I was fighting in transforming my life both domestically and professionally. My wading into the pool of Christianity was also developing during this time; however, I never told a soul—not even Larry. I'd refer to these as my "closet Christian" days. I didn't discuss it with anyone, because of the guilt I felt as a Jew considering a relationship with Jesus.

In 2004, when we decided we would marry, Larry drove past a for-sale sign into a neighborhood in Catonsville, Maryland. The house he found would ultimately become our home. I was leaving behind the predominantly Jewish community I knew. We moved into Catonsville and were married in the living room of our new home in October 2004.

My pondering over Jesus built up in momentum after I moved into Catonsville. The Christian worship songs and my *closet Christian* days seeped into my consciousness, allowing me to imagine myself accepting Jesus into my heart. In these brief moments, I felt *held*. It was a nearly palpable feeling; unmistakable in its presence. He was close. It was intimate and undeniable. I did these ponderings and musings on my own. I shared no conversations with other Christians or Jews, and I didn't even discuss it with my husband. While I believed he'd understand, I was too ashamed to admit *out loud* where I was headed. The weight of the subliminal Jewish message about Jesus that was passed down through the ages kept me silent. More so, I didn't dare tell my mother or siblings about it. How could I? I was a Jew wandering in Jesus' direction and I felt like a traitor. I was still struggling with the condemnation that Jews don't speak or acknowledge Jesus. In many ways, this was holding me back from embracing Him fully. This was the Jesus that our legacy dictated us to never ever consider. To even utter his name was blasphemy, or at least that is what I believed.

In 2006 I turned a corner in my journey toward Christ, and I began to allow myself to consider what it would feel like to be one of his followers. There were several occasions when I'd imagine myself back in synagogue staring up at the starry dome above me. I'd gaze up at the beautiful white vaulted ceiling with its recessed lights beckoning me like twinkling stars. I knew God was up there somewhere. He was far away *watching over me*; of that I was aware and certain. I would compare that distant presence to the nearly visceral connection I felt when I imagined myself in relationship with Jesus, the man. With Jesus I felt held and grounded in God's love. The juxtaposition of this sense of intimacy and intuitive closeness to God as compared to the vacuous disconnect in synagogue was striking.

As I lingered at this fork in the road of my spiritual path in life, the undeniable contrast between my two choices became the impetus to choose the path toward Jesus. It was a no-brainer! An impersonal alliance with God was simply not enough for me anymore. Who wouldn't want an intimate, up front, and personal relationship with the God of the universe! Once I had that silent epiphany, there was no turning back. I had no regrets; no doubts about my decision.

It was at this point that my conversations with my next-door neighbor, Barbara, began to approach more religious topics. Barbara and her husband, Greg, had moved into our neighborhood about four months after us in 2004. Up to this point, we maintained a cordial relationship. I knew that they were *Christians*, but beyond that I mostly kept my distance. One afternoon when Barbara and I spoke in the yard, I tried to convince her I was a *very spiritual person*. I was an *all roads lead to God* kind of Jew. As I turned to walk back to my house, Barbara said to me, "Jill, I'm praying for you." Her words only caused an irritation and discomfort. After all, what did I need prayers for?

Looking back on that moment, I am left with only a deep appreciation for the blessing of her prayers over me. I believe that it was at this point, unbeknownst to me, that my momentum toward the arms of Jesus began in earnest. I also reflect upon the miracle of God's design to have prayer warriors such as these neighbors to move into a home less than thirty feet from my own stone walls.

Within the theater of my new life in my new marriage, I was dealing with my rebellious daughters and a seemingly unending divorce process from my first husband. As the drama in my home escalated, my relationship with Barbara deepened. I found myself leaning on her more for support and prayer and wisdom.

In the spring of 2009, my relationship with my daughters was manifesting an insurmountable amount of turmoil because of the consequences of the unrelenting conflict I had with their father and stepmother. I felt as if I was coming to a crisis point with both of my daughters. Barbara's prayers and Christian-based guidance through the storm became exceedingly important to me. I asked her one night if she knew anything about spiritual warfare. After she recovered from the shock of me even using that particular term, she said, "*Yes!*"

When I asked her to help me with the spiritual warfare between my daughters and me and their biological father, she said, "The only way I know how to conduct spiritual warfare, Jill, is with Jesus."

My response was, "Then its hopeless, because I'm Jewish and I don't do Jesus. I'm an *all roads lead to God kind of gal.*"

Barbara's response to me shook the uncertain terrain I was standing upon. She said, "But Jill, it's not working for you. You've been telling me this for months."

Barbara's words struck their mark within my heart. It was this pivotal moment that began the loosening of the grip of any lingering resistance I had toward Jesus. I agreed to allow her to actively disciple me. We began meeting almost daily as she read passages from Matthew to me. She patiently responded to my endless "yes, but" questions about Jesus and Judaism. She prayed powerfully with me. God had planted an amazing prayer warrior next door to me—what a blessing!

I began spending my free moments with the Bible in mornings over a cup of coffee. I was on the front porch one morning when I stumbled upon the following verses in the Old Testament.

> "*The day is coming,*" *says the Lord,* "*when I will make*
> *a new covenant with the people of Israel and Judah.*
> *This covenant will not be like the one I made*

with their ancestors when I took them by the hand and brought
them out of the land of Egypt. They broke that covenant, though
I loved them as a husband loves his wife," says the Lord. "But
this is a new covenant I will make with the people of Israel after
those days," says the lord. "I will put my instructions deep within
them, and I will write them on their hearts. I will be their God
and they will be my people. And they will not need to teach their
neighbors, nor will they need to teach their relatives, saying,
'You should know the Lord.' For everyone, from the least to the
greatest, will know me already," says the Lord. "And I will forgive
their wickedness, and I will never again remember their sins."
Jeremiah 31:31-34 (NLT)

Out of a stump of David's family will grow a shoot—
Yes, a new Branch bearing fruit from the old root.
And the Spirit of the Lord will rest on him—the Sprit
of wisdom and understanding, the Spirit of counsel
and might, the Spirit of knowledge and the fear of
the Lord. He will delight in obeying the Lord.
He will not judge by appearance nor make a decision based
on hearsay. He will give justice to the poor and make fair
decisions for the exploited. The earth will shake at the force
of his word, and one breath from his mouth will destroy the
wicked. He will wear righteousness like a belt and truth like
an undergarment. In that day the Lord will reach out his hand
a second time to bring back the remnant of his people—
Isaiah 11:1-5; 11 (NLT)

These passages in scripture were like the hidden nuggets I needed
to convince myself that Jesus and God's new covenant with the Jews
was real. My shock at these revelations bordered on outrage at my
Jewish Sunday school training for leaving out these life-altering
passages. It justified any doubts I was having at being *disloyal* to
my Jewish heritage. I began to understand and build my faith upon

the foreshadowing of Christ that the Old Testament was revealing to me.

Some would refer to me as a *Jew for Jesus* or a *Messianic Jew*. I only identified with being *born again*, because that is how it felt. When Friday afternoons would roll around, my TGIF moment was in the realization that Sunday was around the corner and I could return to Grace Community Church and stand in awe and worship of God. I loved standing in the back of the sanctuary so I could watch people standing and singing with passion and enthusiasm for our God. Worship time fed my soul more than any Thanksgiving feast could ever feed my body. Standing in praise of God, arms raised, tears welling as the Holy Spirit moved my heart and softened its walls have become some of the sweetest moments of my life.

◆◆◆◆◆◆◆

I recall a dinner party at my sister's early in my walk with Jesus. A guest at her house was an observant Israeli Jew who knew about my decision to follow Christ. She confronted me with some hostility and attacked my *disloyalty to my people*. She reminded me of the millions of Jews who had died in the Holocaust whom I was turning my back on. I looked her in the eyes and replied, "But now I can pray for them, because I have a personal relationship with God. That's even better!"

HE WILL FIND YOU

He will come near to you if you open your heart.
He will wrap himself around you if you seek Him.
He will light your way if you look for Him.
He will hear you if you ask for Him.
If you knock, He will answer.
Because it is a relationship He craves, He
will wait for you to come to Him.
Hidden deep within the choosing impulse lies
a fertile seed of redemption and glory.
That is why He planted a will within our souls.
So we would ultimately choose to dwell
with Him, in His kingdom.

CHAPTER 21

Reborn

My old self has been crucified with Christ. It is no longer I who live,
but Christ lives in me. So, I live in this earthly body by trusting
in the Son of God, who loved me and gave himself for me.
Galations 2:20 (NLT)

The actual day I accepted Jesus as my Savior was September 13, 2009, at 7:30 p.m. I sat in the living room of my neighbors, Barbara and Greg Hart. They were doing emotional somersaults of joy as I watched in awkward silence. It thrilled them that I had finally agreed to *place my suffering at the foot of His cross.* However, it would be a few weeks later, in the shower, when I sincerely repented and sealed my relationship with Jesus.

But, on this particular day in September, I had reached altitude in my journey. I'd hit the point of no return. Some might describe it instead as *hitting rock bottom.* I had reached a point where there was nowhere else to turn, no one else to speak to, and no place else I could receive relief or clarity from the turmoil and pain in my life. I was metaphorically on my knees, and all I could do was look upward.

It was late Sunday afternoon. I had helped my sister sell her jewelry at a neighborhood crafts festival. On the surface all may have looked normal, but there was a storm brewing inside me. There was a dark cloud amassing strength and a fury that was beginning to surround my life. My youngest daughter had decided to leave me that morning. She was visiting her father for her scheduled weekend. When I awoke on that Sunday morning, I knew she had made the decision. I even heard the words in my mind: *it is done*. As surely as I felt the aches as I tried to stretch out my back as I got out of bed, I knew she was leaving. I can still recall the dark tunnel I entered as I walked into the kitchen for coffee. Larry spoke to me, but I couldn't hear him. I couldn't process anything.

I met my sister a mile down the road at the festival. It was a beautiful September day. One would think all was right with the world, but my world stood in stark contrast to what I believed was everyone else's reality. My life had become one of turmoil and suffering. Larry and I ached as we watched my youngest child transition over several months. She was being urged to leave our home by her father and stepmother. My daughter had convinced herself that life for her would be better living with them.

The process of that transformation, in combination with my own pre-Christian lens through which I looked at life, created an environment that felt like a cold war that manifested as terror. I was in a constant state of dread. Fear kept my stomach in knots and my reactivity to her on high alert. Larry was despondent and felt helpless to change anything. My new marriage was suffering because of my depressed and robotic behavior. In an effort to offer us some relief from our pain, we had bought a precious Scottish terrier puppy a few weeks prior, but I was incapable of feeling any warmth or joy that she offered. I was going through the motions of living. Breathing was the only normal thing I was doing, and that was shallow and constricted at best.

Larry picked me up at the festival later that afternoon. As soon as I entered the car, he and I began arguing about something. I got out of the car, slammed the door, and told him I'd walk home. My absolute rejection of him and my life was as palpable as metal hitting metal as the door slammed shut. I walked the few miles back to my house. I recall the snail's pace with which I did this and the deadened depression I carried through the streets of my neighborhood. The heaviness in my body and soul was so dense that by the time I reached my house, I couldn't go in.

I collapsed onto the bench on my front porch. I couldn't even reposition myself to become more comfortable. My body simply stopped moving, as I toppled onto my side, with my feet still on the granite floor of the front porch. It was an awkward position, but my lying down was not about rest or comfort or ease. It was the embodiment of a complete and total crumbling of body and spirit. The weight that hung over me was so palpable that it felt like there was something else or someone else within my space. I lay there as the otherworldly despair enveloped me like a lead blanket.

I didn't want to go into my house because I knew Larry was in the living room. It was best I didn't go in. I was not alone on the porch in that hour. A dark, heavy presence was beside me. I felt it and wavered between being comforted by it and being pulled into it, as if I felt I was losing my grasp on reality. I hovered in this vacuous space that felt both suicidal and homicidal. Was it my own life I wanted to end? Was it Larry's? He didn't do anything to warrant these dark intentions. I simply recall the weighty presence of darkness and despair and death.

Looking back upon that hour where the enemy cuddled up beside me, I realize how close I came to what the Old Testament refers to as Sheol. Some might refer to it as hell. It was so close to me that I could feel it beckoning me into it. I lay awkwardly on the bench simply aware of its presence. I didn't realize until many months later that it was the enemy or one of its minions.

My neighbor Greg was mowing his lawn. I was vaguely aware of him noticing me lying on my porch. Earlier that morning, I had asked Barbara, Greg's wife, if I could come over that evening to talk. I wanted to tell her about my daughter's decision to leave me and I had hoped to receive Barb's prayer warrior support and solace. She was unable to meet with me due to a previous engagement, so I just laid there on the bench, in the most helpless and hopeless condition I'd ever experienced in my life.

It was about 6 p.m. on this muggy September evening. I'd been motionless in the same position for about an hour when the phone rang. Larry came out to the porch and handed me the phone. Barbara was on the phone and asked me if I was all right. Greg had told her he thought something was wrong. He had seen me from across the front yard and felt the crisis I was in. I told Barbara that something was very wrong. She asked if I wanted to come over. She had decided earlier that afternoon to cancel her plans. By the grace of God, she was free to spend time with me. For the next hour, I waited for her to be available. The minutes slowly ticked away as I anticipated my time with her. I look back on that walk over to Barbara's house as the moment of my life that on an unconscious level I was saying "no" to the enemy.

God gave us a will in order to choose Him. I know this now because I chose life over death on that muggy, cloying September day. I can still imagine the enemy screaming and clawing at me to remain with it in my home, alone and broken. Satan knew he had lost as I practically crawled over to Barbara's house. I was heading to the cross—unbeknownst to me, but well known to the enemy.

Even today, years later, as I sit on a beautiful June morning in my office, I feel the anguish as I type through tear-filled eyes. That moment on the couch in Barbara's living room is still crystal clear to me. The anguish and grief that rolled out of my chest in waves of choking sobs was not only the loss of my daughter, but also fifty-five years of anguish, conflict, and sorrow that were the foundation of my personal journey.

The years spent as a Jewish girl lost and wandering through the desert of my life culminated in my daughter choosing to leave me. The adultery I endured throughout my childhood only set the foundation for the suffering. The events that influenced and shaped me, had brought me to this point of my life where I finally hit an impasse. I was at a crossroads. It took the crisis of losing my daughter to finally drop me to my knees. Barbara could only then say to me, "Jill, you don't have to keep carrying these burdens alone. You can put it all at the foot of the cross."

Through my choking sobs and in a state of complete surrender, I conceded. I spoke one word. "Okay." I remember her reciting the sinner's prayer to me, but it was like a fog. I didn't really feel anything but weighty despair. She said the prayer, and I answered "Yes" when she asked me if I'd accept Jesus as my Savior. Barbara and Greg were giddy with joy as I watched them in awkward silence. They were thrilled that I had finally agreed *to place my suffering at the foot of His cross*. I felt somehow disconnected from them because I didn't feel any joy. It was as if I was outside my body watching them celebrate.

I walked back to my house, and while I didn't feel less depressed, I did feel lighter. I was almost in a daze and was actually too embarrassed to tell Larry what I had just done. I wasn't angry at him anymore but I was feeling self-conscious about my accepting Christ. I thought if I told him about it, he'd see me as just engaging in another drama-ridden intense moment in my life, somehow contrived and insubstantial. In retrospect, this was my own belief about myself. I didn't really believe in myself enough to take seriously what I had just done. I also didn't fathom at the time how my accepting Christ as my Savior would deepen the love between me and Larry over the course of our marriage, but it ultimately did.

It was days later, maybe weeks, that I rounded the corner of this life-altering crossroad when I stepped into my morning shower. This was when Jesus convicted me of the sin of my pride. The shower washed over me as I broke down and sobbed and asked God to forgive me for rejecting Him my whole life. He revealed to me in no uncertain terms how I had spent my entire life trying *to do it myself*.

I believed that my life was all about me controlling every aspect. The *doing it myself* was connected to my pride, which kept Jesus at a distance. The moment was so humbling as I was faced with this sin that all I could do was sob and ask Him to forgive me. These were not tears of sorrow. They were the tears of anguish over the realization of how I had rejected Him throughout my life. How appropriate for Him to firmly convict me and for me to finally allow myself to receive that conviction as the water washed over me and cascaded down the drain.

The crumbling of our walls of pride is a gradual process; at least it has been for me. It continues to be as I cast away more layers of the walls I've built to protect myself. With existential exhaustion, I willingly collapsed into the arms of Jesus on that autumn morning in my shower. With an endless, merciful, and boundless love, He held me and He continues to do so.

And it is impossible to please God without faith.
Anyone who wants to come to him must believe that God
exists and that he rewards those who sincerely seek him.
Hebrews 11: 6 (NLT)

CHAPTER 22

My Baptism

Peter replied, "Each of you must repent of your sins
and turn to God, and be Baptized in the name of
Jesus Christ for the forgiveness of your sins.
Then you will receive the gift of the Holy Spirit."
Acts 2:38 (NLT)

Christmas Eve of 2009 was a pivotal Christmas for me because it was the first time in my life that I celebrated the birth of Jesus Christ as my own personal Savior, rather than the secularized holiday as a wandering Jew. This occurred about three months after accepting Jesus into my life in Barbara's and Greg's living room. While sitting beside my husband, Larry, in the sanctuary at church, I was struck with the urge to seal my commitment to Jesus. Listening to the sermon and singing the Christmas hymns surrounded my heart and soul with such deep gratitude and love that my need to declare this love was something I couldn't deny or ignore. It was almost with a sense of obligation and deep respect for Jesus' sacrifice for me that I decided I was ready to be baptized.

After the mass was over I approached my pastor, Mark Norman, and told him I wanted to be baptized and asked if we could do it quietly in the privacy of his office at some point. Mark smiled with delight as he explained that baptism was not a private affair. Baptism was a public declaration as much for the church body as it was for me personally.

The thought of getting dunked in a bath in front of an entire sanctuary of people was way beyond my comfort zone! But immediately, the Holy Spirit spoke into my fear.

I realized at that moment that if Jesus could suffer and die in front of the whole world for my sake, then certainly I could set my self-consciousness aside and declare my commitment to him in front of my church family.

During this particular time, I was still suffering the loss of my daughter, who had moved away two months earlier. This was my first Christmas without her. The fact that she wasn't speaking to me was a depth of sorrow that felt like a bottomless pit. My continual ruminating on that reality and perseverating on the multiple explanations as to how and why she left me was a deep torment that was relentless. It was a mixture of guilt and regret that wouldn't release its grip from my heart. It's amazing that the Holy Spirit was able to even pierce through this shield of suffering over my heart, and speak truth into it while at church that night.

As I drifted off to sleep that Christmas Eve, my wonderings about Jesus and my decision to get baptized swirled in the spaces of my mind that weren't occupied with my sorrow. I recall awakening from my sleep. It was nearly 1 a.m. when I opened my eyes and was acutely aware of His presence. I could feel Jesus gazing down at me and I began to weep. In my mind and through my tears, I said, "Thank you for dying for me! Thank you, Jesus. I love you. I love you!" My awareness of His sacrifice was so powerful at that moment, all I could do was declare my love for Him. The intimacy of this moment was so thoroughly personal and the depth was so profound that I felt completely immersed in His Holy Love. I felt nestled in His warmth and His breath.

At that moment in his grace and His mercy over my suffering heart, Jesus gave me my Christmas gift. He revealed to me why my daughter had to leave me. Out of respect for the personal nature of my daughter's own turmoil at the time, I choose not to record this revelation in my memoir. I will record, however, that the moment the Holy Spirit offered me this explanation, the vice around my heart opened. The pain and angst I was suffering evaporated immediately. I drifted off into a deep sleep that was the most restful sleep I had had in months. I awoke on Christmas morning with a lightness and a joy I hadn't felt in years.

It took several months for the actual baptism to occur. On August 8, 2010, my pastor immersed me into the water on stage in the presence of the church congregation and even some of my family and friends. My brother drove down from New Jersey to support me. My cousin and his wife were also present, as well as Barbara and Greg Hart, who came along with other friends. Most importantly was my husband Larry and my youngest daughter. This was the daughter whom I suffered over the previous Christmas when God spoke into my heart. It was my conflict with her that finally dropped me to my knees in 2009. She had moved back home a few months prior to my baptism celebration.

For my public declaration, I wore a pair of black leggings and a T-shirt and was invited to step out onto the stage, where my pastor, Mark Norman held my hand and helped me down the stepladder into the tank of warm water. My heart was bursting at the seams with joy as he asked me if I accepted Jesus Christ as my savior. To say "yes, I do" in front of my family and husband was both exciting and empowering. This was my own decision. It was my act of declaration to Jesus. I felt so proud because I knew in my heart I was doing it for Jesus. It was my way of thanking Him and sealing my love and hope in Him and only Him. I could feel the glow of Jesus' smile upon me.

I remember coming back up out of the water and taking my pastor's hand into both of mine and kissing his hand in utter gratitude for playing his part in shepherding me to this point. Looking out at the sanctuary and seeing Larry beaming with joy for me made me giddy. But most of all, I knew I had publicly sealed my fate with the Savior of the universe. I would never go back into the darkness. The parched earth and scorched stump from where I came was part of my past. It would no longer define me or my fate.

I was home.

> *"Out of the stump of David's family will grow a shoot—yes, a new Branch bearing fruit from the old root."*
> **Isaiah 11:1(NLT)**

CHAPTER 23

The Mantle of Regret

You are the light of the world—like a city on a hilltop that cannot be hidden. No one lights a lamp and then puts it under a basket. Instead, a lamp is placed on a stand, where it gives light to everyone in the house. In the same way, let your good deeds shine out for all to see, so that everyone will praise your heavenly Father.
Matthew 5:14-16 (NLT)

Something we latecomers to Christ have in common is a vast landscape of regrets that pool like muddy water under a bridge. Opportunities lost and relationships that were wounded or broken are a constant companion when we ruminate on our lives.

Those of us who resisted His call for too long have a unique challenge when we come to Him later in life. In my case, my children are already grown. My first marriage met its demise. My lost opportunities were already lost.

For me, I sit in church and listen to the stories of families who knew Him during their childbearing years and find comparisons and envy on the flip side of wonder and awe. Latecomers are a subgroup in many ways. I've been a Christian long enough now to know that accepting His hand in no way wipes out sorrow, pain, familial conflicts, sin, addictions, or even falls from grace. What it does do is set a clear pathway toward healing and redemption in which the Holy Spirit will steadily and intimately guide you through.

As a latecomer to Christ, the enemy will always attempt to pull me into that abyss of regret. For me, it's the place where the *if-only*, guilt, and envy can rule the day and wreak havoc on my joy of life. One of the fruits of my growing relationship with Jesus is my strengthening ability to capture these thoughts and dispose of them quickly.

For most of us who did not know Him until later in life, we blundered through our lives as best we could. We completed school, created careers for ourselves, held down jobs, furnished our homes, found another non-believer to marry, had children, and then rinsed and repeated the whole process in one way or another. Some might say that we didn't know any better; others might say that since being saved by Christ, we now are forgiven.

I've been told I was forgiven so many times that it wasn't until several years into my walk with Jesus that I began to understand why those words felt empty. Salvation actually wasn't enough for me. Maybe it was my pride that completely refused to relinquish its influence over my mind, so that the "forgiven" blessings people would remind me about became like water rolling off of a duck's back. It began to irritate me in its emptiness.

My inner voice would cry out, "Yes, but what about my daughters?" or "What about the time lost in my turmoil with my sister?" I lived nearly fifty-five years of my life before Jesus could go to work on me in earnest. I could see my life's horizon with the death of my mother. There was so little time left to become the fisherwoman Jesus had designed me to be!

I was often teased throughout my life that I was a "half empty" kind of person. As a child and adolescent I was a worrier. I perfected my own form of catastrophic thinking during my first marriage. Delving into the depths of sorrows and dissatisfaction was something I was comfortable with. I ponder about these traits as one of the *thorns* that the Lord designed in me so He could ultimately use my weakness for His purposes.

My chronic dissatisfaction with aspects of my life kept me

searching. The rubbing angst and tightening sorrows kept me on the path that would lead me into His arms and His pasture.

I sit here now on the precipice of a new understanding of and freedom from the sorrows. God used the combination of my persevering and overly self-disciplined temperament and seasoned it with my aching envy and jealousies—and even my regrets—to create in me a dogged determination to find an answer. I wasn't aware that I was really seeking freedom from this suffering, but that was the ultimate outcome.

It's a lot like a grain of sand in an oyster. Its continued presence inside the body of the oyster over time gives way to a pearl. The day I began to round the bend in this journey of regrets, I saw in the distance the pasture that He was leading me toward. I began to have enough clarity so I could see purpose in the suffering. Finding a purpose in the suffering of regret is more than finding a reason for it.

A reason for the suffering explains why it haunts throughout one's life, while finding a purpose in the suffering gives it meaning and reveals a direction in life's journey. Most importantly, it offers healing in the process. The suffering begins to take its rightful position beneath your feet. This is not an immediate process, but the process begins once you accept Christ into your life.

When I speak with other latecomers to Christ, I discover that we share a common sorrow. But I also find that we share a common passion. Our gratitude for Jesus saving us is so stunningly alive that our walk with Him is in a permanent state of technicolor rather than black and white. It's strikingly 3-D rather than merely one-dimensional. I'm not suggesting that those biologically born into a Christ-filled family or who walked with Him throughout the bulk of their lives do not feel a similar passion. I'm only suggesting that the regrets that come with too much time lived without Him also offer a poignant and striking intensity that can frequently overwhelm and drop you to your knees in utter gratitude and love.

The juxtaposition of life before and after being born into Christ has a continual presence in the minds and hearts of latecomers. If this juxtaposition awareness was a separate living organism, then mine sits beside me at worship time, breathing on its own and nudging me repeatedly. I am reminded continually of the scorched stump I was born out of.

For Jesus to wait as patiently as He did for us to surrender into His arms is simply overwhelming to ponder. That He gently and lovingly nudges us and woos us with such forgiving persistence is stunning! For Jesus to quietly shepherd us into His pasture without us realizing it or appreciating His protective guidance is beyond comprehension!

As a mother, my deepest regret in looking back was not raising my children to know and love Jesus. Had I known Him intimately as I do now, there are so many things I would have done differently. Had I known Him when I divorced their father, I would have walked through that particular experience with so much more grace than I was capable of at that time.

"Lack of grace" is putting it mildly. Without Jesus in my heart, I spent nearly a decade after my divorce in fear, anger, angst, and hand-wringing worry. My daughters were the most immediate recipients of all that brokenness, and there are no do-overs. The suffering my children had to endure over those years shaped them. While they knew without any doubt that I "loved them bigger than the sky," which I told them when I'd tuck them in at night, they also knew my short temper and my fragile fear as I clawed my way to redesigning my new life.

As I round this particular bend of my journey and ponder the mantle of my regret regarding my children, God reveals the way for me. He knows, as do I, that the most valuable impact I can make on my children as their mother is to lead them into His arms. He and I know that discipling my family by urging them to join me on this Christian journey would only alienate them. I can only disciple to them by living in intimate communion with Jesus. By keeping Him close to my heart, He will reveal Himself to them. It feels subtler, but it's no less powerful.

Latecomers to Christ will invariably come to this same crossroads. It's the born-again Christian's dilemma. The intense desire to bring loved ones to Christ is tempered by the realization that being overt about it could push them further away from Him and you. Latecomers to Christ struggle with an intense level of passion and purpose and a heartfelt need to save our children and families who do not know Him. The pang of helplessness is a gnawing, persistent longing; it can be a very lonely experience.

In my journey bearing the mantle of regret, the Holy Spirit finally clarified, in no uncertain terms, that my children did not belong to me. They belonged to Him. With this conviction came the guiding directive that it was through my countenance that I was to disciple to my loved ones. My children and my immediate family would see Him through my transformation. It was through my own sanctification that they would come to know who Jesus was, whether consciously or unconsciously.

In this revelation, I could see the possibility of putting down my mantle of regret. The grief that gripped my heart like a vice over these muddy waters began to loosen. He had in some ways released me from my self-constructed responsibility to fix my life and undo the mistakes I had made. The Lord reminded me that He wouldn't have taken me this far to drop the ball and leave me to wander alone. He wouldn't have transformed me and leave my most precious loved ones untouched. My hope lives inside that promise.

His promise to guide me eternally would include the beloveds in my life. My daughters and my family would come to know Him through witnessing my life, not necessarily through my words or teachings. My words and teachings would only be machinations of my pride. He had given me permission to nail my pride to the cross. He had given me permission to bask in the glow of His forgiveness.

The regret that clung to my soul like ivy to a tree had kept me vigilant and aching. It kept me on a path that only He knew about. It was an intimate journey between Him and me. He knew where it would lead me, while I only knew the suffering. While I only knew guilt and a sense of helplessness over my loved ones, Jesus promised me His faithfulness. He loved me in spite of myself and my mistakes. By nailing these regrets and sorrows to the cross I began to be able to place even these burdens at His feet. I could leave my worry about my life and the destiny of my daughters and my family with Him.

Regret began to transform into a ministry of purpose and loving determination to allow Jesus to keep guiding me with my daughters and my family. The Holy Spirit could love them through my hugs and my laughter. The Holy Spirit would listen through my ears. His heart would resonate with their hearts through mine. I see how in so many ways He loves them and protects them on a daily basis. When I pray, He reassures me they are front and center to Him. He uses me to entice and attract them into His arms.

I am His ambassador. The millisecond of time that I walk this earth, I pray fervently on their behalf. This sacred intercession, this mantle of regret, becomes transfigured into a call for action. Only a Holy Love could set this ambition with such passion.

As Christians, we pray for our families, but as latecomers to Christ, our mantle of regret fuels an urgent determination and passion that smolders endlessly just below the surface of our countenance. It's a visage that the Holy Spirit has shaped for us. The Holy Spirit holds that space on our behalf.

We are the warriors at the border of our loved ones' territory. Jesus guides us into His arms so we can pave the way for our beloveds' ultimate destination—His loving embrace.

CHAPTER 24

The Mercy of God

*"And I will forgive their wickedness, and I will
never again remember their sins."*
Jeremiah 31:34 (NLT)

In June 2009, three months before I gave my life to Jesus, I felt compelled to bring my mother to Grace Community Church one Sunday. My hopes were for her to listen to my pastor Mark Norman preach, and hear the worship music to see for herself what had drawn me in.

I had told her I was contemplating a relationship with Jesus and I'd been going to the Sunday services since March of that year. The compulsion to bring her on that particular Sunday was very powerful. It had a driving force of its own that I didn't understand.

Even though it was challenging since she was in a wheelchair, I managed to get her to the church that morning. Mark Norman's sermon was on King David's adultery, Psalm 51. Only the Holy Spirit would have moved me to insist that I bring my mother on *that* particular day!

My mother at the time was eighty-one years old. She had taken to living predominantly in her bed because of her chronic pain from progressive scoliosis, spinal stenosis, and osteoarthritis. My mother was wheelchair-bound, dependent on others to prepare her food, help bathe her, pay her bills, and clean her house.

She appeared to enjoy Mark's sermon. What she understood

about Psalm 51 I'll never know, but she asked me to arrange a meeting between her and Mark. I introduced them that morning at Grace Church and she flirted with Mark, as only my mother would do. Mark in all his graciousness agreed to meet with her at a pre-arranged time.

This meeting took nearly six months to coordinate, given the pastor's schedule and my mother's homebound condition. Mark helped by offering to meet with my mother at my home one blustery day in October 2009. I picked up my mother and brought her to my house and got her settled. She sat comfortably in my living room near the large bay window. The view was my wooded backyard. Bushes were swaying in the wind, and leaves were blowing around the yard. Mark arrived with a big grin and an open heart.

I brought in tea and cookies and prepared to leave them alone, but Mark suggested I stay. That disappointed me because I had hoped and anticipated that if my mother had some private time with Mark, she would repent and admit her failure as a mother. I would finally get the apology I'd yearned for my entire life. What happened was much better. I witnessed a miracle; an unexpected and astonishing one!

I sat on the couch as Mark proceeded to share the story of the gospel with my mother. He described who Jesus was and explained His status as the Son of God. He described the reality of salvation and the blood of Christ; that Jesus had died for our sins. He explained how Jesus was the *once and for all* sacrifice. This is not what I anticipated and I was shocked! She was Jewish. She was a sweet woman but her depth of character or capacity for complex intellectual concepts was never apparent to me in my lifetime. Her capacity for abstract conversation was never evident, at least not to me. I recall one day when she was in a rehab center following a brief hospitalization. I brought her a little card that had the word "grace" on it. She looked at it and said, "Who's Grace? I don't know any Grace. What's this for?" I spoke to her of grace, but I'm not sure she grasped the concept.

I couldn't imagine how she could understand or grasp the magnitude of what Mark was offering her. Mark finally asked her if she wanted to accept this gift of salvation. He explained that because it was a gift, she needed to actually accept it. He gestured with his teacup, demonstrating that she had to accept the cup in order to drink the tea. Accepting Christ was the same idea. She had to accept His gift. He explained that any relationship is a two-way street. There is a give and take. God wants us to want Him.

God wants a personal relationship with all humanity. He planted our wills within us so we could ultimately *choose* Him. God does not want robots. He wants real lovers.

My mother looked at him and after a few moments of silence, said, "Sure!" I knew she didn't really understand the priceless value of the gift she had just said "sure" to. I assumed she was only being polite. As Mark began to recite to her the sinner's prayer, she interrupted him. She said, "Excuse me, but look," and she pointed out the window to the boxwood bushes and blowing leaves. She stated that she saw people clapping, laughing, and dancing outside.

My mother was not delirious, hallucinating, or demented. She was not delusional or psychotic. As I watched the leaves blowing, it was as if she watched *the angels rejoicing*. Looking out that window, my mother had a vision that only Christ could have blessed her with. Mark was grinning broadly as he told me the angels rejoice every time a person comes to Christ.

In the same way, there is joy in the presence of
God's angels when even one sinner repents.
Luke 15: 10 (NLT)

This striking afternoon was the destination that the Holy Spirit was guiding me and my mother toward in that funeral parking lot many years before. In the summer of 2006, He told me my job was to 'save my mother spiritually.' God had used me to bring her to this moment so that my pastor could guide her the rest of the way.

Because of my pastor, my mother was saved. Because of his intervention on that blustery October day, I came to understand that God loves us so much, He'd forgive and embrace anyone. He forgave the adulterer, King David, and He was even willing to forgive my adulteress mother. As shallow as I believed my mother to be, God knows that what she gave to Him was everything she had to give. Her "*sure*" was the very best He would get from her in the flesh, and her "*sure*" was enough.

> *"You don't have enough faith," Jesus told them. "I tell you the truth, if you had faith even as small as a mustard seed, you could say to this mountain, 'Move from here to there,' and it would move. Nothing would be impossible."*
> **Matthew 17:20 (NLT)**

My mother loved me with all her heart. It just wasn't enough for me. It was a maternal love that was so shallow and so broken, it left gaping holes in its wake. Her legacy is impoverished and fallow. Yet within that emptiness, God would reign supreme in the end. Through witnessing her salvation and the divine vision she described, I was able to understand who God is and His willingness to forgive. I could begin to understand His mercy.

My mother didn't deepen her relationship with Him in the following three years of her life, at least not that I could discern. There was no spiritual fruit that I witnessed during the remaining three years of her life. Nevertheless, one day, several months after her coming to Christ, we had a brief conversation. I had stopped by to pay her a visit and found her in her bedroom sitting in her wheelchair facing her blank TV screen. Her caretaker had gotten her out of bed for a couple of hours. My mother turned to me and asked, "Does God forgive naughty girls?"

"Of course He does," I said. I asked her why she'd asked that.

She said, "I think I've hurt people." I asked who she thought she hurt. She said, "I think I hurt your father." I knew in that instant the Holy Spirit had indeed whispered truth into her heart. The light of His truth had pierced her own dark secrets. When God convicts us it is always out of love. Maybe that's why she was able to, in her own little girl way, receive it.

I finally had the chance to say what I had wanted to say to her my entire life. I told her that she did hurt him, and she also hurt my sister and me. We sat in silence for a period of time. Then I suggested to her that I believed that the physical pain she had to endure from her spinal stenosis may have a lot to do with the sorrow and regret she might be holding onto.

We sat in a prolonged silence again. It reminded me of my patient from Montebello Hospital when I sat vigil while the Holy Spirit did its work with her. I suggested to my mother that if the pain inside could be talked about, and *see the light of day*, then she might have some relief. If she could ask for forgiveness, then forgiveness could be given. Nearly five minutes passed as she stared ahead at her blank TV screen.

And then I saw it. A tear slowly slid down her cheek. That tear was the closest thing to an apology I would ever receive. Her words that followed were heartbreaking. She said, "The pain is too deep." I imagine that for a mother to fully acknowledge the devastation she had caused her children, it would sear one's heart like a hot knife. Maybe her tear also revealed sorrows that were concealed in her own memory vault. Sorrows that I never knew about. Sorrows that were etched into the wall of her own soul. My mother was a woman who danced intimately with secrets. I had to acknowledge that her life history was not accessible for me to ever fully know. Who knew what events and fears and hurts she clung to and tucked away from the light?

Her nursing aide then walked into the bedroom and broke what felt like a spell. That breath-stopping moment helped me to feel compassion for my mother's silent suffering. It was the first seed of what would eventually allow me to forgive her for the sorrow she had caused me and my sister.

◆◆◆◆◆◆

> *Love is patient and kind. It is not jealous or boastful or*
> *proud or rude. It does not demand its own way.*
> *It is not irritable, and it keeps no record of being wronged. It does*
> *not rejoice about injustice but rejoices whenever the truth wins out.*
> **1 Corinthians 13:4-6 (NLT)**

The fruit of that afternoon with Mark and my mother in my living room, as we looked out that window, was the fulfillment I experienced in being obedient to God and helping to co-choreograph my mother's salvation. That experience helped me begin to understand God's mercy and grace and the extent of His love and forgiveness for us all.

For me, the resulting fruit that was produced from that experience was the promise of hope for the rest of my family. I love them all so much and want them to know the Lord personally! There are so many facets of this miracle on that day. As I journey on with Christ, I receive even more revelations about His grace and forgiveness. And as my faith grows, He continues to reveal more of Himself to me. There is still so much work to be done, so much healing, so much forgiveness, and so much grace.

> *Create in me a clean heart, O God. Renew a loyal*
> *spirit within me. Do not banish me from your presence,*
> *and don't take your Holy Spirit from me.*
> **Psalm 51: 10-11 (NLT)**

THE SEED OF FORGIVENESS

Nestled deep within my awareness of her
brokenness and unintentional destructiveness lies
the seeds of my forgiveness for my mother.
Forgiveness is part of the journey I am on.
Forgiveness cleanses the soul.
It restores the heart to its God-given capacity to love.
To love again is what I seek,
like a drowning person seeks the light,
knowing that oxygen comes with it.

CHAPTER 25

The Pain Was Too Deep

*"I have told you all this so that you may have peace in
me. Here on earth you will have many trials and sorrows.
But take heart, because I have overcome the world."*
John 16: 33 (NLT)

Yesterday God spoke to me in church. He revealed to me that
as He used Judas He used my mother. In her sinful life, He
allowed her to carry a pain that only a mother could know. If a
mother were to fully acknowledge the devastation she caused her
own children, she would have to endure her own deep guilt. The
suffering around that would be unbearable.

I know the times I've caused my daughters pain. While never
intentional, there were many times that my own pride and unresolved
personal issues influenced my behavior. My anger or fear would
dictate my reactions to circumstances so that there'd be interactions
with them where I'd miss the mark at best or say something hurtful
at worst. As I've grown in Christ and seen the fruits of healing
relationships with my daughters, the guilt has given way to purpose
and determination. This healing guides me in the many interactions
and opportunities I now have to love on them.

But as I sat in church under the shadow of His conviction
yesterday, I was face-to-face with the remnants of my self-righteous
judgment toward my mother. God used her and her sinful life to
raise me up to hunger for His protection and love. I doubt that I'd

have had such an insatiable appetite for Him had I not been the daughter of my beautiful, adulteress mother.

I know now that she carried pain that was too deep and too locked within her to even allow it to see the light of day. Maybe her suffering in the latter bedbound years of her life was the physical manifestation of the deep burdens she carried. She sealed her sin in worldly terms, but He forgave her and welcomed her into His kingdom, anyway. I know that's why the angels rejoiced at her shallow acceptance of His gift that afternoon with my pastor, Mark Norman, and me.

At that moment, when she said to me, "The pain is too deep," I was a witness to the kingdom of God's truth. When someone speaks truth that has His fingerprint upon it, one can experience the vastness of God. It's like standing on holy ground. It's palpable, just like my memory of that moment in her bedroom. For me, the one tear that rolled down her cheek was her apology I had hungered for. She was not able to utter the words or even look at me. But I saw her pain, and I felt the depth of her suffering; authentic and profound in its power and darkness. It was without a doubt the only time in my entire life with my mother that I experienced sincerity and pure truth. In that moment, I saw her suffering with crystal clarity. The tragedy was that her secrets were concealed so deeply and so tightly that all she could release was one tear. It was as if her pain was locked inside with no way out.

It was the first and last truly authentic moment I'd ever share with her. There were no expectations or agendas; no role reversals or co-dependency. It was a moment of pure honesty. Even though she didn't look at me or elaborate, I chose to believe that the silence and weightiness of that moment was a result of her love for her children and for my father. I can recall that moment and rest in beginning to understand that my mother's love for me was deep and pure, but concealed in a dark place. Her actions always tainted and tarnished her maternal love, and I never knew its purity. But I can hold on to that moment, which manifested the timeless bounds of her love as God designed it. He allowed her to take His gift of maternal love and ruin its sweetness, but He didn't remove it. I witnessed it that afternoon.

In that quiet conviction as I sat in church yesterday, I felt my heart begin to soften toward my mother. As a result, I saw a purpose in her sin and in my suffering. I saw the bigger picture. In the bigger picture, God's plan is revealed. In those milliseconds of mercy, where He will give me a glimpse of His vision and plan, it alters my life. I know that He parcels out these moments from His own timeless reality. He is so amazing! He sections them out because, in my smallness, it would blow me away if He let me linger inside His revelation beyond a certain amount of time. It's too overwhelming for my mere mortal self to bear. Maybe it's unnecessary as well. Because God is so big, it takes a seemingly minuscule moment to change one's world.

Writing this book is part of why He allowed my mother to be who she was. In my journey from innocent victimhood, to my brokenness, and through the years of my pride, He called to me and waited for me to allow Him to lift me out and up into His embrace. The journey toward healing and forgiveness is a universal one. He designed us to be forgiven and to forgive. Forgiveness is the key to opening the vault that contains love as God designed it. Grace is the key to Holy Love.

His mercy extends for the big sins, like my mother's, and also for the little daily sins in our relationships with all of our beloveds. We are all sinners. We are all ruled by our own pride, which has its grip on our ability to love each other with all of our hearts. How often does a spouse disappoint us? How often do we not *get* our own children and miss the mark? The hurts pile upon each moment; and without the art of learning to forgive, we limit our capacity to fully love. Forgiveness and love are an intimate dance like the yin and the yang, and the tug and the pull. It's a beautiful waltz if we allow it. It's a dance that can sweep us up into the realm of Holy Love. Holy Love belongs to Jesus. He gifts it to us as an inheritance and He helps us to learn the steps…to master the dance.

Not only so, but we also glory in our sufferings, because we
know that suffering produces perseverance; perseverance,
character; and character, hope. And hope does not put us
to shame, because God's love has been poured out
into our hearts through the Holy Spirit,
who has been given to us.
Romans 5:3-5 (NIV)

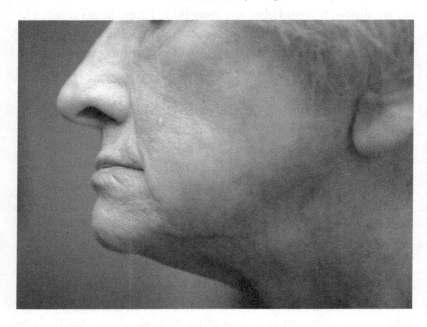

CHAPTER 26

Eulogy to my Mother

And forgive us our sins,
As we have forgiven those who sin against us.
Matthew 6:12 (NLT)

My mother died on December 10, 2012. She collapsed by her bed at home from a stroke and died on the way to the hospital. The funeral was held at a Jewish funeral home in Baltimore County. I was given an opportunity to speak in front of the sanctuary of guests and mourners. After reading the account of how my mother accepted Christ, with me and my pastor on that blustery October afternoon in 2010, I read the following eulogy:

Monday night, I found myself saying goodbye to my mom.

I'd imagined that so many times in my mind in the last couple of years, but when that time actually arrived, I was simply stunned. All the emotional imagery was only a fantasy. Monday night, the reality was surreal.

I sat with her with my eldest daughter beside me for nearly two hours as we waited for Levinson's Funeral Home to come to pick up her body. I didn't want her to go to the morgue. She wouldn't want that. It would have terrified her. She'd be all alone in that cold darkness.

When Levinson's came and said I could leave, I said, "No, I want to stay." I wanted to watch them wrap her up and securely tuck her away in the hearse. Watching it might make it less surreal and possibly take this numbness and turn it to pain.

Then I realized that I wasn't doing this for Mom. I was lingering and stretching out the time I had left with her. I didn't want to let her go. I didn't want it to be over.

On Tuesday night, the day after she died, I went to her apartment on the way home from work as I have done for the last few years. I sat on her bed where she lived the last years of her life. I held her pillow to my face and just breathed in. I've done this with my daughters' pillows when they've been gone for any length of time. Did you know that the sense of smell is the most primitive of our five senses? The olfactory nerve goes directly into the emotional part of our brain. No detours. I'd breathe in the pillow, and I could feel my children, and now Mom.

Driving home, I had to ask myself, what is this thing? What is this pull that makes a daughter not want to say goodbye to her mom?

Motherhood is not an easy journey. It's the most enriching and the most powerful experience, but it can also be the most heart-wrenching. No other experience will demand more from a woman. We all make mistakes as mothers. God knows I've made mistakes.

Mom made mistakes. I'm not going to lie about that. It wasn't easy being her daughter. There was sorrow, and there was angst.

But why after all that would I be unable to walk away from her on Monday night? Why would I want to breathe her in one more time?

God designed something that is woven into the fabric of motherhood—unconditional love. He planted unconditional love and forgiveness into our hearts. It's the unconditional love that shines beams of light into the shadows so you can see the sweetness too.

I can see her laughing. I see her singing. Mom loved to sing, and she had such a beautiful voice! I see her teaching me and my sister songs. I see us in my brother's bedroom dancing to the Temptations and Gladys Knight. I see her teaching me how to dance funky and sexy. I see her and Dad dancing in the living room at one of their parties. I see people gazing at my mother as my family was escorted to our table at a restaurant. She was so beautiful! I imagined that they thought that Marilyn Monroe had dyed her hair black and walked in.

In the chapter of Luke (15:10), we learn that whenever someone accepts God's gift of salvation, the angels rejoice. I'm so grateful that because of God's unconditional love for all of us, He has also forgiven my Mom, and that she is with Him in the freedom and the fullness He designed her for from birth. I'm so grateful she is not suffering anymore.

If I were asked, what my mother's life was about, and what is the most important gift I've gotten out of being my mother's daughter, I would have to say that it was knowing unconditional love and forgiveness. And for that, I am truly grateful.

Eulogy, Dec 12, 2012

For a child is born to us, A son is given to us. The government will rest on his shoulders. And he will be called: Wonderful Counselor, Mighty God, Everlasting Father, Prince of Peace. His government and its peace Will never end. He will rule with fairness and justice from the throne of his ancestor David for all eternity. The passionate commitment of the Lord of Heaven's Armies will make this happen!
Isaiah 9: 6-7 (NLT)

CHAPTER 27

Story Shared

Confess your sins to each other and pray for
each other so that you may be healed.
The earnest prayer of a righteous person has
great power and produces wonderful results.
James 5:16 (NLT)

About a year after the death of my mother in 2012, I felt
compelled to share my story with my pastor. My pastor listened
intently and patiently as I relayed my secrets to him. When he finally
spoke, his first words were, "Jill, the only word that comes to my
mind as you speak is: "*tragic*." His words jolted the foundation of the
dam that was bearing the weight of a sorrow palpable in its power
and density.

Then he said, "That must have been so hard for you!" His words
were so simple, but they shook me to the core. The dam cracked and
I burst into such deep sobs that I could barely talk. My head ached,
and I thought I'd pass out from the force of this furious wave of
grief. I cried out, "It was *so* hard!" As I sobbed, I felt like a seven-
year-old little girl again, who's weeping congealed into a mass of such
profound sorrow, there were no other words left to speak.

As I cried, he took out the Bible and opened it to Ezekiel 16.
Ezekiel was a prophet who spoke for God around 570 BC. In this
passage of Scripture, he is reminding the Jews from where they
came and how God had deeply loved them from their infancy as a

nation of His people. The message in Ezekiel 16 is about how Israel prostituted herself rather than live in righteousness. In the broader picture, Ezekiel 16 lays the foundation as a foreshadowing as to why God had to come to humanity as Jesus. The Ten Commandments and the legalistic Jewish culture were not enough for the Jews to maintain their righteousness. God wrote the laws in stone. Jesus would ultimately create a way to plant the laws in our hearts.

> *But you thought your fame and beauty were your own. So, you gave yourself as a prostitute to every man who came along. Your beauty was theirs for the asking. You used the lovely things I gave you to make shrines for idols, where you played the prostitute. Unbelievable!*
> **Ezekiel 16:15-16 (NLT)**

> *Then you took your sons and daughters—the children you had borne to me—and sacrificed them to your gods. Was your prostitution not enough? Must you also slaughter my children by sacrificing them to idols? In all your years of adultery and detestable sin, you have not once remembered the days long ago when you lay naked in a field, kicking about in your own blood.*
> **Ezekiel 16:20-22 (NLT)**

> *Yes, you are an adulterous wife who takes in strangers instead of her own husband.*
> **Ezekiel 16:32 (NLT)**

The adulteress Israel was part of my story in its Jewish legacy and in my family of origin. My pastor and I talked for nearly an hour, after which he prayed for me and my family. He prayed for my forgiveness of my mother. I was not ready to forgive her. That came some years later.

As I left his office, he added that I also needed to forgive myself. As I drove home, I pondered that last statement. I was the victim!

What did I have to ask forgiveness for? I pondered that even as I placed my head on my pillow that night.

I had colluded with my mother. To align myself with her, I cooperated in hiding her indiscretions from my father. I lied to my father for her sake. I whispered messages into her ear from her assortment of lovers, as she sat beside my father watching TV. When she received a phone call from a man, I discreetly informed her. Whether my father knew what I was doing, I'll never know. But it's this man, my beloved father in the flesh who has been gone since 1984, whom I seek forgiveness from.

I believe that it was by the grace of God that somewhere in my mid-teens, I stepped back from that sad arrangement with my mother. I recall standing in the hallway and facing my mother when I said, "I'm not doing this anymore." She and I didn't speak for weeks.

In addition to my beloved father, I also needed to confront my own resistance to Jesus. As I lay there in the dark that night, reminiscing about my father and my mother and our pathetic familial dance, I suddenly became aware of the tattered teddy bear doll from my childhood.

I could envision myself gripping that doll even now as a grown woman. That doll symbolized my dream of a perfect childhood with a perfect mother. My image of my mother was still of the sweet, funny, beautiful woman whom I loved. That image was not the adulteress or the destructive mother. The doll symbolized my childhood, my fantasy, and my lifelong wish for something different. Inside that doll lived my victimhood. My sense of myself as victim fueled my anger, bitterness, and grief. My victimhood kept me broken, and it also kept me stuck.

More importantly, inside that grip and unrelenting idolization of my imaginary family life was a resistance to Jesus. I was resisting Him. In that moment, I knew that if I let go of my dreamlike doll, Jesus would be there. In my refusal to let go, I was refusing to let Him adopt me completely. I had to let go of the idol of my perfect mother in order to grab onto Jesus' hand.

It was my pride and my need to travel the journey on my own that I needed to repent of. I needed to ask Jesus to forgive me for my own self-protected stance.

I let go that night as I drifted off to a peaceful sleep. That night, my relationship with Jesus began to deepen. I had stepped beyond the children's shallow pool into deeper waters.

Lord, my heart is not proud; my eyes are not haughty. I don't concern myself with matters too great or too awesome for me to grasp. Instead, I have calmed and quieted myself, like a weaned child who no longer cries for its mother's milk. Yes, like a weaned child is my soul within me. O Israel, put your hope in the Lord—now and always.

Psalm 131: 1-3 (NLT)

CHAPTER 28

Anatomy of Shame

But I will call on God, and the Lord will rescue me.
Morning, noon and night I cry out in my distress,
and the Lord hears my voice. He ransoms me and keeps me safe
from the battle waged against me, though many oppose me.
God who has ruled forever, will hear me and humble them.
Psalm 55: 16-19 (NLT)

Parental abuse, or even misuse, in the absence of a sincere apology, can become fertile ground for the damage and suffering that follows.

In the case of my mother's adultery, my foundation became fertile ground for a shame that permeated every cell of my body. The role reversal that she required of me had no *turn off* valve. I carried the shame that is the stain from a life within the heart of adultery. I experienced my shame with a self-disdain that was always lurking beneath my conscious awareness...until it would rear its ugly head. Whether it came as a grade that was anything less than an "A" in school from grade school and through two graduate schools, or to an acupuncture patient who terminated their treatment with me, or an interaction with my children where I *missed the mark,* and anything in between, the shame and self-disdain were the immediate response on my part. At those times, I'd pull into myself in a depressed state. In my twenties I often contemplated suicide but was too afraid I'd muck up the attempt and live in some brain dead or crippled state.

The diagnosis that my numerous psychotherapists landed upon was a "dysthymic disorder" or "anxiety neurosis." These were labels I settled comfortably into in the search for an identity. It justified the nearly fifteen years of psychotherapy I sought out in my search for a relief from the gnawing discomfort and bouts of depression.

If my mother had ever, in the course of my life, looked me in the eye and acknowledged her indiscretions and destructiveness, and sincerely apologized, I'm certain that would have been life-altering for me. In the absence of her acknowledgment of the damage she'd inflicted upon me and my sister, it left me with the only possible outcome…the visceral belief that I was irrelevant and insignificant. This was the most damaging part of all. I'm sure she would have denied this; but in those formative years for me as her daughter, the dye was cast. My existence took second place to her relationship with other men. This theme permeated her relationship with me throughout my childhood and well into my adulthood and up to her death in 2012. This sad reality set the stage for what became my quest for relevance and love.

◆◆◆◆◆◆

In 2010 a blockbuster movie called *Avatar* hit the theaters. A scene between the blue heroine beauty and the conflicted part human/part avatar hero struck a chord within my heart. He had wandered back into her world and found her looking for him in a beautiful forest. He was uncertain if she would accept him back into her life. She looked at him and said, "I *see* you." At this point in the movie, it was obvious to all that she was in love with him. By saying "I *see* you" she was declaring her love out loud. This was how the beings in her Avatar world expressed their love in words.

The power of that moment finally made sense to me when I began writing my memoir. For a person to see into the soul of another, the sin and the righteousness, the good and the bad, the failures and the triumphs, and to still love that entire person, was striking to me. In the theater it took my breath away. Jesus loves all of us that way! He sees everything about us; the good and the bad, and he loves us still!

> *O Lord, you have examined my heart*
> *and know everything about me.*
> **Psalm 139: 1 (NLT)**

In 2015 as I began to record my life, it spotlighted a profound truth. Love for another human being in our life was about seeing all of them and wanting to be with every aspect of that person. This is how God designed it, because as it says in Psalm 139, the Lord knows us fully and loves us eternally. It is like setting a laser beam directly into the heart of the other person and seeing that Holy place where God dwells. Even though we may not yet have a personal relationship with God, this *laser beam* is by His design. To be seen in this way is the result of love that reaches far beyond the passion of the flesh. It extends beyond the worldly expectations of our relationship with a spouse, or a son or daughter or sibling. To be seen in this way lands one into the arms of Holy Love. My first moment witnessing the speaking of Holy Love on the big screen left me breathless.

Years later I can understand on a much deeper level why not being seen by my mother was so devastating. A mother's love becomes part of one's foundation of who they are, and why they are. It's their *home base* that becomes the lighthouse of comfort and soothing. It contributes to the foundation of one's own identity. In the absence of being *seen* by my mother, I was left wanting. I was left up to my psyche's attempts to construct an identity and meaning to my existence.

I filled the gaping holes with the enemy's constructs. Depression and anxiety, as well as catastrophic thinking, along with several years of panic attacks were my symptoms to suffer. Shame and the self-disdain that were its handmaidens took hold. Reflecting back on the journey as my mother's daughter, I recognize the impact that these constructs had on my capacity for deep, lasting friendships with women and men. I recognize the isolation and withdrawal from others as the only reliable and consistent comfort zone I could have. I recognize the stunting impact on my sense of my own sexuality and sense of myself as a woman.

Understanding the power of the irrelevance and insignificance I felt as my mother's daughter illuminated the reality of my sense of invisibility. Shedding light on that tragic conclusion laid the foundation that would allow for healing to begin.

The clarity that resulted from this healing process helped me to understand part of the anatomy of the shame for a victim of abuse or even misuse. The actual violation that is the hallmark of the abuse is what causes the initial wound. Silence from the offender sets the stage for the festering of a wound that simply cannot heal. Lack of acknowledgment of the abuse and seeking forgiveness is dishonoring to a victim's dignity. This absence creates an emotional vacuum and sets the stage for more destruction. An identity of victimhood sets in and roots itself into one's soul. With that comes the flourishing of the sense of irrelevance and insignificance. Shame proliferates like weeds that line a highway. Hopelessness feeds off of the sense of irrelevance and has no relief. Relief can only come with an acknowledgment of one's humanity that creates an opening for forgiveness.

Forgiveness is the key to healing. To forgive in the absence of my mother's apology required nothing less than me taking hold of my own God-given relevance and significance. I had to use my own God-given will to direct myself forward, taking responsibility for my life and heart. When I allowed Jesus to step into my life in September 2009, I began this healing journey in earnest. It was not immediate. In fact, it took nearly another decade to turn the corner and emerge from that particular parched valley.

There was no way I could have done this on my own. The years of psychotherapy only outlined the issues. Stopping there would require me to think my way to healing, which is woefully inadequate if not impossible. Only Jesus could step into this mess within my soul. Only His love and strength could direct my will to recovery and cleansing on that deep level that no years of psychotherapy could excavate.

He will rescue the poor when they cry to him;
he will help the oppressed, who have no one to defend them. He feels
pity for the weak and the needy, and he will rescue them. He will
redeem them from oppression for their lives are precious to him.
Psalm 72: 12-14 (NLT)

CHAPTER 29

Tale of Two Mothers

For I was born a sinner—yes, from the moment my mother conceived me. But you desire honesty from the womb teaching me wisdom even there. Purify me from my sins, and I will be clean; wash me, and I will be whiter than snow. Oh, give me back my joy again; you have broken me—now let me rejoice. Don't keep looking at my sins. Remove the stain of my guilt. Create in me a clean heart, O God. Renew a loyal spirit within me.
Psalm 51: 5-10 (NLT)

I became a mother on March 11, 1990. By the grace of God, I became pregnant very easily with both of my daughters. Becoming pregnant seemed effortless for my body. The physicality of motherhood was easy and healthy for me. The love I had for my daughters and the innate urge to mother them was the first real taste of womanhood that I could claim as my own. I would repeatedly play Carole King's "You Make Me Feel Like a Natural Woman" while I breastfed my babies. Up to that point, I'd never felt such a sense of completion in my life. The love I experienced when holding my babies in my arms defies words. It felt euphoric and boundless. The desire to merge with my daughters was profound, and breastfeeding lulled me into a peaceful reverie. I'd waft their powdery fragrance and stroke their satin skin.

It turned out that for me, the motherhood journey beyond their infancy was another story altogether from the *imaginings* of what I thought it *should* be. As my daughters began to grow beyond my maternal grasp, I began to re-experience an all-too-familiar ache. I felt disappointed. The possibilities for frustration were infinite. To name a few of the many motherhood challenges, they might scream too loudly, refuse to eat, or refuse to wear the outfit I chose for them. By defying my desires or not meeting expectations of how they should be, I began to sense a shift from Holy Love to cerebral love. The lifelong walls and defenses I had erected with ironclad protection began to resurface.

It was like waking up from a wonderful dream while trying your hardest to recapture the images and feelings, only to blink as daylight sets in, illuminating reality. It was like reaching into an ocean and trying to hold on to the water, but it slips effortlessly through your fingers. My experience of motherhood became tainted like that scorched pot of soup of my own childhood.

Maternal love was satiating to me until my daughters would anger or frustrate me in some way. Then a sour taste would return, and I found myself missing the sweetness. I was incapable of holding onto the pleasantness in the face of the normal challenges of motherhood. These challenges were simply the typical frustrations of all mothers; universal issues that everyone deals with while raising another human being. I, however, was incapable of walking through this tumultuous phase of early motherhood with the grace I would have hoped for. The demands of an overcontrolling spouse with its accompanying unforgiving tension, along with typical and endless domestic challenges were like border walls to my joy and peace.

The persistent ups and downs of life and mothering created an underlying gnawing awareness that my capacity for love was fractured in some way. I would try to deny this because of my own harsh self-judgment. In many ways, it recreated the experience of my own childhood. I was reliving and recreating from my childhood my sense of deception and shame. A sense of fraudulence and inadequacy permeated my spirit throughout this phase of my life.

In many respects, my daughters saved my life. My relationship with them sounded the alarm of my brokenness. But, like hitting the snooze button on the clock by my bed, I'd return to my slumber, incapable of fixing myself or knowing how to take any action.

Could I hide it from them? Could I conceal it from others? I looked like the perfect, doting mother on the outside, but much of the time I was either numb or in turmoil because of my crumbling marriage. It's no surprise that my first marriage was doomed. How could anyone with my family history and lack of self-worth be capable of identifying a loving match? How could anyone with my background be competent to love a spouse well? I chose an extremely controlling man thirteen years my senior. I believed he would save me from myself and my history. Yet I was clueless at that point in my life that being saved could only come from Jesus Christ, who was not even on my radar screen at that time. These were those self-righteous *all roads lead to God* days. Coping with this phase of my life and trying to be a better mother and wife was up to me and my series of psychotherapists. In retrospect, this was all woefully inadequate.

I muddled through the motherhood years of two little girls and navigated my way through the divorce from their father. As a single mother, I reinvented my career as a nurse and entered a graduate school of acupuncture. I remarried in 2004 and started my life over with my daughters. Had I not stumbled into Jesus' arms in 2009, I tremble at the thought of how my relationship with my daughters would have ended up.

The decade following my decision to divorce their father sent my relationship with my two precious little girls into a tailspin. As a parent, navigating our children's adolescent years is challenging at best. Having to do this during a tumultuous and adversarial divorce process sent me and my daughters into deeper waters that we were not prepared for. That, nearly, ten years of my life, hold some of my deepest regrets.

Accepting Jesus as my shepherd and Savior has offered me the possibility of freedom from the pain of those regrets. It's not that *being saved* is like a lobotomy. No one can cut out that part of my memory from my brain. I still occasionally wince when I revisit those years in my mind. But the juxtaposition of who I was in those years as compared with who I have become now as a born-again Christian gives me a continual impetus to journey on as I perfect my ability to love my daughters well, as God designed.

Search me, O God, and know my heart;
test me and know my anxious thoughts.
Point out anything in me that offends you,
And lead me along the path of everlasting life.
Psalm 139: 23-24 (NLT)

CHAPTER 30

A Mother Reborn

Humans can reproduce only human life,
but the Holy Spirit gives birth to spiritual life.
John 3:6 (NLT)

It's stunning; the contrast of my life with my mother juxtaposed upon my life with Jesus.

Jesus embodies love. He *is* love. He is the embodiment of selflessness. Jesus gave all of Himself—every last drop of His worldly and royal essence—for the sake of my life!

In contrast, my mother was the embodiment of selfishness. I speak this without anger, and as I speak it, I still love her. She was my mother.

My mother was sweet and funny, but she was the ultimate self-absorbed mother. We were only reflections of her. She imposed her needs upon her daughters from early childhood, throughout our lives, and up until her death. I never knew my mother to not be involved in an affair, both during her marriage and after my father's death. I remained a dutiful, well-conditioned daughter throughout her life and even up until her death as her body was driven away in that hearse on December 10, 2012.

Except for her protecting me as a baby and toddler, there are too few memories where I could entrust my life into her hands. She met my physical needs, but there were too many moments in my life when the needs of my heart remained exposed and vulnerable.

I do not mean for this to sound bitter. The bitterness and anger are both gone. What is left is the simple fact that my life was one that journeyed through a desolate valley emotionally.

My mother's shallowness and selfishness left no room for her to give of herself for the sake of her children. I know she loved us with all of herself. But it was a self with meager depth.

In contrast, Jesus gave everything He had for the sake of my life and yours. The image of Him hanging limp and completely emptied out on the cross is the personification of Holy Love. As I reflect on Jesus, I turn my gaze to my relationship with my two precious daughters.

The only way I can love my daughters well and push my own worldly needs out of the way is through Him. There was no possible way I could love my daughters well, on my own. I am my mother's daughter, after all. I need Jesus to walk beside me to keep me on the path of motherhood to nurture my adult daughters and our relationship. Only the Holy Spirit can show me how to selflessly love while maintaining a standard that can guide them.

I turn my gaze upon Mary. Her assignment was to love, protect, and raise Jesus in the flesh. But in her devotion to God, she released her son when he was of age. She released Jesus to do God's work. What am I to learn from her?

Mary was the embodiment of maternal love and faith; maternal love and sacrifice; maternal love and obedience to her Lord.

I sit here with these moments of clarity, despairing over a conflict with one of my daughters. And in a heartbeat, God convicts me. He reveals to me that my despair is really all about me, and not my daughter. I am loving my daughter as a citizen of this world.

When God despairs over me, it's all about me and not at all about Him.

Father, please help me to love my daughters as a citizen of Your kingdom! To love my girls in holiness is to release my white-knuckled grip on my expectations. It's loving them with open arms, without

*grasping. It's loving them without imposing my will. They are
adults now, and I pray that you will help me to guide them the
rest of the way. Please teach me. Guide me and strengthen me to
be like Christ as I mother my daughters into their adulthood.*

In the journey toward Holy Love, Jesus will reveal to us our
own sin first. The defenses and walls that our own pride erected and
which impede our loving as He designed are what we need to see.
The weightiness of my own pride is palpable. I can't seem to distance
myself from it sometimes. It feels so much like it's a part of me.

Maybe that's part of my conundrum. Holy Love is how God loves
us. Only He can love that way. We are mere imprints of that love,
the verb of that love. But we can strive to become its manifestation
and live and love in the glow of His Holy Love…His warmth…the
eternity that He created and that He dwells within.

In faith, I will wait for that promise.

Is my *seeking* for that Holy Love what He wanted from me all
along?

I know He does not want me to make an idol out of the seeking.
This is a narrow pathway that He shepherds me on.

Reaching for Him, and seeking out Holy Love…it's like a
continual seeking of Him. The Holy journey toward God.

Just the mere knowing it is there is enough. In God's grace and
in His Mercy, He revealed it to me in glimpses. An assurance that it
is indeed there, like appetizers before the actual banquet.

So, I will not waver. I will stay steadfast on this narrow path…
because I am headed straight into His kingdom!

*My old self has been crucified with Christ. It is no longer I who live,
but Christ lives in me. So, I live in this earthly body by trusting
in the Son of God, who loved me and gave himself for me.*
Galations 2:20 (NLT)

THE PUREST GOLD

The purest gold is only forged from the hottest heat.
As the heat dissipates in the forging process, the resulting gold
that is left becomes the precious metal whose value is timeless.
The heat of worldly passion can be like a supernova exploding.
It's brilliant in its splendor, but it pales in comparison to
what it can become as a relationship is shaped over time.
My mere mortal self keeps clamoring for the heat and
the brilliance…but my heart whispers to me:
"Seek the gold."

CHAPTER 31

Musings on Motherhood

*Place me like a seal over your heart, like a seal on your arm.
For love is as strong as death, it's jealousy as enduring as the
grave. Love flashes like fire, the brightest kind of flame. Many
waters cannot quench love, nor can rivers drown it.*
Song of Songs 8: 6-7 (NLT)

The journey into the realm of Holy Love is one of deliverance. It's a journey that can only be experienced through struggle. In the struggle is the tug and pull; resistance dancing with embrace. The tension and the dance build our own spiritual muscle to endure and persist over time. It's the magnetic pull that all human relationships are called to. The yearning for connection to one another. It can only come with a relationship that is so significant that the stake it has in our lives in the flesh is high enough. It matters—sometimes, too much.

*Yes, the Sovereign Lord is coming in power. He will rule
with a powerful arm. See, he brings his reward with him
as he comes. He will feed his flock like a shepherd. He will
carry the lambs in his arms, holding them close to his heart.
He will gently lead the mother sheep with their young.*
Isaiah 40: 10-11 (NLT)

The sanctity of motherhood and marriage; these have been my pathway to Holy Love. Their power over me is what offered the purification process that was required for my deliverance onto that distant shore.

The dark and the light, the yin and yang, the tug and pull, the back and forth, they create a tension. And only through that can we build the muscle of the heart to prepare it for that sacred space that He prepares for us, His design for Holy Love. As I sit here in my sixties, I feel—often with anguish—the finiteness of my time here on earth. Since the passing of my mother in 2012, I've sensed the dissolving of a buffer that concealed my own mortality from my awareness. That horizon looms over me like a shadow sometimes. I feel the diminishing time here, and the anguish of that simultaneously illuminates these moments of Holy Love with such bright clarity.

The blessing is found amidst this solemn awareness.

> *Give thanks to the Lord, for he is good!*
> *His faithful love endures forever.*
> **Psalm 118: 1 (NLT)**

There is a point in our mothering where the path we are on with our children diverge. They will continue their journey separate from us. In actuality, their path is always separate from ours. As mothers, we know the piercing reality of separateness once they breathe air on their own in that chaotic delivery room. Amidst blood and water and tearing flesh, we rejoice at their cries and their new life.

Our journeys intertwine like ivy wrapping itself around the trunk of a tree. Our paths parallel so intimately that we as mothers forget that they are indeed separate from us. As Christian mothers, we know in our hearts they don't belong to us. But as women of the world, we forget and deceive ourselves into thinking we are still attached by that lifeline cord. There comes a point where we can deceive ourselves no longer.

The fruit of the mother-child relationship has the sweet flavor of affection. The heart of the mother is beating love, and it can flow out to her child and intermingle with their own flesh and spirit. There are valleys along this journey where, sometimes, the path cannot bear the fruit we would wish for. Sometimes, the path is a prodigal journey for the child.

What then?

God designed motherhood and pregnancy. Sin designed labor pains. God designed the fruit of the motherhood journey, but God allowed the sweetness to turn sour when sin stepped in. Motherhood does not guarantee sweet fruit. We long for it, and we grieve over any lack of it. We forget that our children belong to Him first and to us second. We forget that they have their own journey that they will have to navigate in the world.

There is a point where our paths diverge, like a fork in the road. The map is not clear. We don't have an aerial view as to the outcome or its landscape, but as Christians, we do have hope. Hope is the fruit of our choosing to love God first and everything and everyone else second.

At that moment when I demand that my path with my daughters remain intertwined, I, on an emotional level, re-experience the agony of labor. When I demand my right to remain attached to them, to have control over their lives, and keep my absolute right to a cornucopia of sweet fruit, I suffer the hunger pangs that promise to leave me wanting.

There are passages in this mothering journey where we simply can't taste the sweetness. These are through the life dramas and conflicts, the misunderstandings, and the prodigal detours. The enemy would hope to deceive us into thinking our love has gone stale. The enemy would have me feel those hunger pangs and conclude that the love bond has moved from my heart to my mind only. This would have been my former story before I knew Jesus.

Thank God for Jesus! He surrounds this relationship with His warrior angels. I know that it was only through Jesus' compassion and mercy that He strengthened my stance to remain undeterred when my flesh was screaming to let it all go.

> *I am counting on the Lord; yes, I am counting on him. I have put my hope in his word. I long for the Lord more than sentries long for the dawn, yes, more than sentries long for the dawn. O Israel, hope in the Lord; for with the Lord there is unfailing love. His redemption overflows.*
> **Psalm 130: 5-7 (NLT)**

There is a difference in surrendering my daughters to God and holding on in love. They are not mutually exclusive, but rather in harmony.

I sit here meditating on God, and as usual, my thoughts turn to my daughter and our past tumultuous relationship. I write this as I reflect back on the past turmoil with my daughter during her adolescence. The vision I have of her and my relationship with her back then is that we were out in the ocean in a storm. The tempest raged and the waves smacked me in the face, stinging my cheeks. I was holding on to this rope, but I couldn't see her at the other end, and yet I knew she was there.

There was no joy in any of this. It was dark and cold. The waves were relentless and merciless; the salt burned my eyes.

At that time, this mother-daughter relationship was not sweet, gentle, or kind.

So, while I surrendered her to God, in faith I continued to pray for her protection and for God to guide her into His fold, and to not forsake her. I surrendered my white-knuckled grip, while not letting go of the rope. The rope is the eternal cord of motherhood.

There are times in this motherhood journey that maternal love comes down to this single, bare tether—all that is left, incapable of being severed; the bedrock of forgiveness and love.

MOTHER WARRIORS

So, what is a mother to do when her prodigal daughter
stays distant in that far-off land of hers?
A mother waits because her love and the bond are eternal.
What is maternal love?
A mother waits…her swollen eyes turn to You for solace.
A mother waits…her aching heart opens
to Your breath as she hopes.
Patience can only come from You when our arms
ache from remaining outstretched, longing for
our prodigal child to return into our arms.
We watch from the distance that they put between us.
We wait because we are mothers, and that's what we do.
Sweet Jesus gives us the strength to be still with open hearts. He
warms the protective shield we had to place over our hearts.
The enemy uses our prodigals to weaken our resolve
to maintain our stance and our open arms.
Jesus will have none of that!
With the Son we stand firm and strong!
"I am counting on the Lord; yes, I am counting on him.
I have put my hope in his word…. For with the Lord
there is unfailing love…" Mother warriors are we.

CHAPTER 32

Motherhood and Surrender

*Then Jesus said to his disciples, "If any of you wants to be my
follower, you must give up your own way, take up your cross,
and follow me. If you try to hang on to your life, you will lose
it. But if you give up your life for my sake, you will save it."*
Matthew 16: 24-25 (NLT)

Surrender usually conjures up a forced condition. It seems
shrouded by conflict, fear, helplessness, and feelings of being
overpowered. However, with Jesus, surrender is something we
choose. In that surrender, we find our strength. That choice on our
part is what allows Christ to step in and strengthen our ability to
release our grasp on the things of the world. As Christians, we know
that this is neither an easy nor an immediate process.

Surrender in love to Christ gives birth to those open arms of
release, as we crucify ourselves to the cross along with our love for
Jesus. We as mothers can begin the Holy journey of motherhood
anew. This is a daily practice that has its origins in the love we have
for our children.

But how could I possibly do this until I discovered Him face-
to-face with His arms stretched wide open, beckoning me into His
embrace? How on earth would it be possible to forego my flesh and
pride when my mortal self was screaming to hold on to my daughters
and my former role as their mother? This was the only role I knew

and was the role I contrived out of my childhood distress with my own adulterous mother.

Releasing that fleshly bond reminds me of the story of the woman bound and shackled in a shed by a serial rapist. She found an ax and cut off her own foot to release herself and escape. That is my only image of what it would be like to release my emotional grasp. To surrender my motherhood experience to Christ felt like an insurmountable sacrifice.

But with Him in my heart, where I finally allowed Him to reside along with the Holy Spirit transforming my mind and soul, I witnessed miracles beginning to happen. He transfigured on the cross, and I allowed Him to do the same with me.

Recalling that pivotal day back in my office in 2009, His voice said, "You were never here to mother them in the flesh. You are here to love with holiness, as Mary loved Jesus." That was the week that my daughter decided to move out of our home and in with her biological father. There had been several gut-wrenching confrontations between us that preceded the final decision on her part. This had culminated with His voice to me in my office.

It was September 15, 2009. I had made it into the acupuncture clinic to work that morning. When my colleague at the front desk saw me walk in, she said, "You can't greet patients looking like that. Go into your office and pull yourself together!" I knew that the psychiatric hospital was only half a mile away, and I was considering driving there at the end of the day and voluntarily admitting myself in as a patient.

I felt as if I was losing my mind. Nothing made any sense. My world had tilted on its axis, and my broken heart felt as if it had ceased beating. I gazed out the window onto the highway, immobilized.

That's when He whispered into my heart and revealed to me that the quest for Holy Love is what my life was about. In that millisecond, my life flashed before me—the lack of maternal security, the adulterous dramas of lies and deceit, my mothering experience fraught with angst, and fear of a controlling, demanding husband and interfering people in my life. I had neither the capacity nor the will to push back on the enemy's use of other people in my life that disrupted my role as my daughters' mother. I couldn't learn how to mother with the strength and grace I yearned for.

As a mother or a woman, I had no self-confidence. My childhood legacy and my former marriage had made their mark. I only had a frail, pathetic sense of insignificance in relation to my children. This was what God spoke into at that moment in my office. This desolate, scorched-earth space is what God breathed into. It was in that instant that the pain and heaviness lifted. It would take several years for me to fully grasp what He had said to me and to see where He was taking me. What He said in that moment gave me a sense of comfort in its clarity and truth. It was like salve on a burn; a balm on a severely wounded soul. Maybe that is why the pain persisted for several more years. The agonized dissatisfaction, the gnawing guilt, the persistent unrequited longing…it all kept me searching. It kept me on the path He was shepherding me to.

I've been a mother since 1990, and I sit here today in 2015 and realize that for the first time in all these years, I am gazing out on the pasture that He cultivated for me. It's now several years beyond that day in my office in 2009. Coming into the light of His pasture was painful and gradual, sometimes so subtle as to be imperceptible. My daughter returned home to me about six months after she left. She was emotionally wounded and spiritually spent. We spent the next many years healing our wounds both individually and together as mother and daughter.

Love endures—my love for my children as well as Jesus' love for me. My determination to stay on His path has become unrelenting. As I strengthened my resolve to grow as a Christian, my strength as a mother in my heart and mind and toward my daughters grew. As the blood of Christ washed me, my self-doubts and distorted view of myself as a mother began to surge away, allowing God's design for me to emerge shiny and new.

What felt agonizing at times is what kept me searching and prevented me from settling into a complacent *as good as it will get* place in worldly terms. It kept me longing for something more. I no longer could detach and depersonalize from the hopelessness I had as my mother's daughter. The passion to love my children well, inside and out, had become front and center in my life, and Jesus would not allow me to settle for anything less.

I am grateful for the agony and the self-doubt that permeated my motherhood journey because without it, I would not have yearned for the greener pastures and still waters that awaited me. The possibilities of what my daughters and I can share from this point forward are glorious. I see it—finally! From subtle glances at each other to striking moments of laughter, or even disagreements or grief shared, the possibilities of what we can share now with hope and promise are endless.

It is in that hope I declare, "HALLELUYAH!"

Out of the stump of David's family will grow a shoot—
Yes, a new Branch bearing fruit from the old root.
Isaiah 11:1 (NLT)

SHOW ME THE WAY

Show me the way, Jesus.
Shepherd me into the clearing…into the light that is Your creation!
I get a glimpse…a flickering of clarity…a moment in the clearing.
I see it!
There is hope in that moment, because I get a snapshot
of where You are taking me…and I know it is real.
I can only see it with my heart. But how can I put that into words?
A blood cell rushes through the heart, and then
it courses through the rest of the body.
It's like that—the vision, the clarity. Here one
moment, one beat, one breath—then gone.
But there is hope in that breath. It will return. There is hope.

CHAPTER 33

The Pain of Pride

*This means that anyone who belongs to Christ
has become a new person. The old life is gone; a new life has begun!*
2 Corinthians 5:17 (NLT)

As my faith in Jesus strengthens and my relationship with Him deepens, prayer becomes the salve on days of fear or anxiety. Whether these dark days are because of issues that arise with my daughters, or my husband and myself, or my work, or beyond the walls of my home to my siblings or community or country, prayer has settled my heart and given me peace.

I would welcome the moments of conviction, when the Holy Spirit would speak into my heart and I would hear His corrections He was making to my character structure. He'd point out a flaw in my manner of responding to my husband, or an area of selfishness, or how I needed to alter some way I was dealing with my daughters or my sister. Convictions from Jesus were remarkable because guilt was never the response on my part. From a loving father who only wants the best for me and loves me beyond my comprehension, His convictions never produced guilt. They only produced change.

One of the most life-altering moments of His convictions of me was on the highway as I drove my daughter home from visiting my thirty-four-year-old former stepson. She made a comment to me that revealed her distorted belief about me and how she was told I had conducted myself during the divorce from her father. As

I white-knuckled my steering wheel attempting to restrain my rage and my insatiable, unrelenting need for her to *know my truth* about the divorce process, the Lord stepped in. He knew the war raging in my heart over the battle I was having around my daughters and their father. He knew my intense need for them to *choose* me over their father. To love me and trust me more than their father was a righteous battle that hummed continuously within my soul in those years. Rage and bitterness fueled this battle. In a millisecond, Jesus set me on a different path, beyond the war-torn battlefield I tended to like a well-watered garden.

It was as if Jesus took my face into his hands and forced me to gaze into my conduct with my children. Demanding that my daughters choose my truth and my reality was only hurting them. My need for them to turn to me as their sole source of parental love and guidance and sustenance was all about my own needs. It was my pride that was dictating my conduct. This pride of mine had nothing to do with their welfare, or their hearts or their pain. It was the antithesis of my maternal responsibility toward them. The charge of motherhood is to love and protect the welfare of our children.

To love my daughters *like Mary loved Jesus* would require nothing less than me putting down this mantle of pride around the divorce and their loyalty to only me. It required me to sacrifice that banner I was holding high in my mind and heart. Loving my children well should be about them and not about me. In some respects, this decision to change course with them and for them was the biggest sacrifice of my life.

Guiding them into adulthood so they could discover truth on their own began to guide my conduct as their mother. By stepping away from that battleground I had nourished, I gave my daughters the space they needed to find their own way with their father and stepmother. The space between their father and myself was like a demilitarized zone of an ongoing war. There was no love or safety in that space for my children. My attachment to the *war* became strikingly clear when the Lord stepped in and convicted me on that day. In a mere moment, my perspective shifted from me and my prideful need to see their father *lose* this war, to the welfare of the heart and minds of my children. Putting down that battle cry within my heart felt like nothing less than a sacrifice of paramount proportions. It was my first glimpse into God's design of Holy Love as a sacrifice.

Only Holy Love has the power to suck the oxygen out of fire that powerful. The bitterness and rage that unfortunately can flourish amongst divorce battles can develop a life of its own. Without Jesus leading me, there was no way I'd have ever seen the error of my way, and how I was hurting the two human beings I so cherished. There was no way I could have ever thought my way to this new vista. Without Jesus' strength, I couldn't walk this new path with my children. It felt like a very narrow path because multiple opportunities would arise where my prideful need to *win* would rear its ugly head. The Holy Spirit would pull me back onto His path and help me *stay on track*.

Over time I settled into a peaceful place of acceptance that my *win* would have become their loss. I understood that my daughters aligning themselves with me, at the exclusion of their father, would have been an empty victory. They would have missed out on a relationship with their father; and it would have also developed into a bittersweet alliance with me as their mother. If I had the welfare of my daughters as front and center of my maternal stage, then my job was simply to love them and hold that space for us as our own family unit. Then their relationship with their father had its own time to bloom in its own way. Their relationship with their father and stepmother had nothing to do with me. Amongst the fragrance of this more peaceful place, my relationship with my daughters could heal and begin to flourish as the Lord designed it.

Another area of growth that Jesus guided me in was in releasing the white-knuckled grip I had on my relationship with my daughters in general. They were indeed separate from me and loving them well was about allowing them to find their own way in their adult lives.

By aligning myself with Jesus, I felt secure and peaceful enough to allow my motherhood role to blossom. As the angst and rough edges of a war-torn divorce battle abated, the ensuing calm gave way for trust to redevelop between my daughters and me.

No psychotherapy or cognitive therapy or self-help books or acupuncture treatments could create this transformation. No chanting my way into oblivion could do it. A cerebral understanding did not initiate these changes, nor did my will alone accomplish it. The God of the universe initiated them, moving my spirit and softening my heart, so that my mind could follow suit. It was only Jesus stepping into this mess that gave me the ability to begin to experience the rewards of loving well. As a Jewish mother who found her way into Jesus' arms, I can celebrate both my own journey toward redemption and the mother-daughter(s) relationship that was beginning to flourish.

I prayed to the Lord, and he answered me. He freed me from all my fears. Those who look to him for help will be radiant with joy; no shadow of shame will darken their faces.
Psalm 34: 4-5 (NLT)

A HEART THAT HAS OPENED

Because of my hardened heart, I was able to know
the difference when it began to open.
When the armor began to melt away layer by layer.
Only the heat of the Holy Spirit could accomplish this miracle.
A sealed-off room with its dank and musty thickened air...
The seal on the window seams begins to crack and fray.
Chips fall away over time.
Time.
Suddenly, the window opens and the light blinds.
The crisp air pierces the thickness and stagnation.
The chest hurts with expansion.
The ice is breaking.
Crisp and clean.
Cool and refreshing, with the warmth of the sun's rays.
Yes, I know the difference!
The gift in the suffering is this astute perception.
It's the ability to feel the difference
between loving through my will
and loving with my heart.
One is love going through the motions.
The other has the glory of His kingdom imprinted all over it!

CHAPTER 34

Recovery

My old self has been crucified with Christ.
It is no longer I who live, but Christ lives in me
and gave himself for me. I do not treat the grace of God
as meaningless. For if keeping the law could make us right
with God, then there was no need for Christ to die.
Galatians 2:20-21 (NLT)

I am left asking myself what to do with my broken heart and all my regrets. I can choose to wear them like a badge of honor, allowing them to define me. This choice would inevitably continue the legacy of dysfunction in my own new marriage, and into the hearts of my children and beyond. Or I could, by the grace of God, move on. I believe that these are choices we all share because we all have wounds within us.

In my journey toward redemption, I've come to realize that I am seeking to come as close to Holy Love as possible in my millisecond of this earthly existence. I know that the gift of the suffering I endured and fanned the flame of is responsible for this quest toward Holy Love.

The years of self-disdain, alternating with depression and anxiety, are giving way to the ability to sustain my gaze into my own sins. Whether if it's about my temper or times when I judge others, or my insensitivity or detachment—to name a few—I am becoming capable of seeing who I am. I can see these parts of myself that exist hidden in tiny nooks and crannies of my soul. I can sustain my gaze upon them because I'm accepting that Jesus also sees these sins, and that He loves me anyway. There is no longer any need to hide. Jesus gives me the strength to turn my gaze away from my history so I can look at myself honestly. In these painfully honest moments with myself, I can surrender once again to my Creator. As I turn in Jesus' direction, I can begin to see me as He sees me...the good and the bad.

The enemy can't live in God's light. In those darkened corners of our psyche, the enemy revels in coexisting with us. The enemy must remain hidden in order to do its work to keep us from coming closer to God's design for our capacity to love in holiness.

In realizing over and over how much I need an intimate relationship with God and His ongoing forgiveness, my attachment to Him strengthens. My surrendering to Jesus allows His light to shine into my darkened spaces, as His roots grow deeper within my heart. This Holy light cleanses anything in its path!

As I surrender to Jesus' love, I realize that even my shame is merely a fabrication of my own pride. To linger in that space is actually an indulgence. Its like dancing with my self-defined identity. It's what I created within my own mind. What pains Jesus most is not only my sin, but these prideful maneuverings that keep Him at a distance. With Jesus in closer proximity, I can step aside from the shame and self-disdain and lean into His light. This alternative is the answer to finding joy and contentment in my life. As I depend on His strength to be better and love better, I can learn to be a better mother, wife, and sister. I can even take a more loving path with my nieces, nephews, friends, and neighbors. There is no limit to what a heart that is finally open can offer the world. With Jesus as my partner, there are no limitations to loving.

Whether it is with my husband, my daughters, or my siblings, I'm coming to a place of clarity. Jesus is revealing to me the layers of fabricated stories we face each other with. If, for example, my relationship with Larry was a dance, then we are belly-to-belly with our own stories that we each bring to the dance. These layers of self-protecting stories keep us from dancing heart-to-heart. Jesus designed us for a heart-to-heart love, not belly-to-belly love. Mastering the intimacy of *that* dance is why we are here.

Holy Love is that sweet space where there is no longer any space between two souls. We will all ultimately get there, to that Holy place with our beloveds; that place where the love connection is sustained eternally. No more sorrows, no more stories, and no more layers of prideful protections.

Heaven on earth is those Holy moments when we make heart-to-heart contact with our beloveds. If we are seeking it, with Jesus as our Shepherd, He will reveal the way for us.

As an acupuncturist, the Holy Spirit has taught me sometimes to gaze in a subtly shifted direction away from the point I am trying to find on a patient's body. It's an indiscernible shift to the naked eye. If my patient were watching me, they wouldn't even notice that my gaze was away from the acupuncture point. In these moments, it is the Holy Spirit's hand that guides my fingers and places them on the very spot He intends me to find. It's like He is saying, "Trust me, Jill. Let me. I've got this."

We can do the same with our own lives. We can will ourselves to "take this on" and can train ourselves to discern His voice. It's like a shift in gaze.

The woman whom I loved deeply, my mother, was the same person who broke my heart. Her infidelity and legacy of deceit left me wounded and beyond the repair of my many psychotherapists. God has used my battered life and my ability to disconnect as a way of protecting my heart. My tendency to disconnect haunted me and distorted my self-image my entire life. It also gave me the ability to be transparent without regret as to how others might view me. It's only God's view of me that really matters.

Years ago, I discovered a card in a bookstore that stated:

"WHERE THERE IS SORROW THERE IS HOLY GROUND" (Oscar Wilde)

"You are too serious. You worry too much." These were the mantras that were repeated to me throughout my life. Why couldn't I be lighter-hearted? "Your cup is always half empty" was the criticism that hovered around me as I journeyed on. "You're too deep," I was told. "I never met anyone who needed something to be *real* more than you!" As I look back and reflect, I began to see sorrow as a gift that I would dance with throughout my life. The sorrow kept me searching. It kept me suffering and dissatisfied. It kept me seeking, and led me into His arms. The suffering is what ultimately overtook me and dropped me to my knees at the foot of His cross. This was the place where my true recovery began.

> *The LORD says, "I will give you back what you lost*
> *to the swarming locusts, the hopping locusts,*
> *the stripping locusts, and the cutting locusts."*
> **Joel 2:25 (NLT)**

HOLY LOVE HAS NO NAME ON IT

Holy Love has no name on it.
It has no boundaries.
You can find yourself immersed in it and not feel lost.
In fact, you feel the most secure and joyous you've ever felt.
It's like the first time you hold your baby.
You think it's about him or her and their
tiny hands and their tiny feet.
And their sweet fragrance.
You are lost in it and you are found, simultaneously.
We think it's about the other human being
that has touched our lives.
But no.
It's about His breath that he has gifted that person with.
God's ways are beyond our understanding.
Holy Love has no expectation. No conflict. No conditions.
It has no layers of complexity that weave the
fabric of the human belly to belly dance.
It consumes the space that once contained oxygen
and fills it with something so miraculous
and so lovely in its magnificence
that like the flickering candle or the raging fire,
it will find common ground within which
to surround you with warmth.
To share a moment in time with another
or even a few other people
where His love has entered the space
is a blessing that can only come from God.

CHAPTER 35

Bedrock

Therefore, this is what the Sovereign Lord says:
"Look! I am placing a foundation stone in Jerusalem, a
firm and tested stone. It is a precious cornerstone that is safe
to build on. Whoever believes need never be shaken."
Isaiah 28: 16 (NLT)

Holy Love is clean love. It's pure in its truth. It's authentic in its display. There are no layers of the worldly turmoil that befalls all human relationships—the layers that settle into the space between your heart and the heart of another. It's simultaneously simple and overwhelmingly boundless.

What is the bedrock of motherhood? Where is that place in our relationship with our children that only truth and love exist? It is different for each of us and for each individual relationship.

I had a moment last week when the clarity of my love for my mother struck me like a lightning bolt. It was a *God moment* and stunning in its power. These moments are life-altering when they come unexpected, when you are not even looking for them. You may think the stars were all aligned in the right position at that particular nanosecond, or you may think you had a fever so your defenses were down. I know that the Holy Spirit works in mysterious ways and that our understanding is not like His. I attribute these life-altering moments to Him.

In this particular *God moment*, I lay in bed reading a novel about a Scottish man who was about to place the pebble onto the tombstone of the daughter he never knew. They buried her in America. However, they erected a tombstone in her honor in Scotland, as well.

In a sudden flash, an awareness penetrated my heart. For the first time in too many years, possibly for the first time in my life, I missed my mother. The sudden need to touch my mother's headstone was palpable, as if touching it would feel like I was touching her. There were no thoughts outside of my flood of tears and an ache in my chest. All I knew at that moment was that I wanted my mom. I wanted her unconditional love. There weren't any thoughts at that moment. There were only feelings and amorphous images. The awareness of my bond with my mother was foundational. It was as if I had settled onto firm bedrock and I could sit there in that space of love with my mother.

The woman who was my mother was profoundly flawed and too self-absorbed to mother me in a way that would allow me to flourish; but at the most basic and authentic layer of reality, she was still my mother. As her daughter, I loved her, needed her, and missed her loving me in return.

I was so deeply struck by this awareness that all I could do was put down my book and curl up beside my purring cat and sob. I sobbed until my head ached and my eyes burned. My whole being ached with the desire to touch her, and sit in the glow of her unconditional love. There was no thought about her indiscretions or the endless missed opportunities and selfish choices she made. In this moment, any sadness, resentment, or feeling of loss was missing. All that was left was the maternal bond, the bedrock of it all. It stunned me that it was there all along, beneath layers upon layers of worldly disappointments.

It had been four years since her death—four years' worth of holidays and anniversaries of her death; all of them were just another day in my life regarding my mother. I had never returned to the cemetery to visit her. I had no desire to go there, and I had never missed her or thought much about her. But, at that moment, the years of burdens she had placed upon me dissolved. The only thing that remained was the truth. It was the bedrock of maternal love; that tether of motherhood that is unbreakable and unchangeable. On that firm foundation, I stood in wonder and awe as I realized that the love we shared was, indeed, real and pure. As a result, I returned to the cemetery to place a pebble on her stone, a Jewish ritual, and to be with her, as her daughter.

As a journeying Christian, I've come to realize that there are certain states of awareness and insights that I can't think my way to. Nor are there some conflicts I can think my way out of. I have to allow the Holy Spirit to shepherd me there. He took me to the heart of healing on this particular night alone in my bedroom with Luna, my cat.

The journey to healing is ongoing. Coming to this place that night was like arriving at a pasture He would allow me to rest in for a time. To linger in this place in my mind and heart was His act of mercy and grace. A balm, a nourishing moment that felt timeless. It could sustain me as I picked myself up and sojourned onward toward other pastures. I could move forward, less broken and with less hurt than before.

In His mercy, He revealed to me that loving maternal bedrock that was Holy.

For God has not given us a spirit of fear and timidity,
but of power, love and self-discipline.
2 Timothy 1:7 (NLT)

ON DISAPPOINTMENT

The enemy will take our disappointments in our loved ones and
fan that flame so that it will overtake us and consume us...
until it eclipses our love connections
and we will forget...as if asleep...
and as if in a dream,
it becomes our reality in those wee hours of the night.
The disappointments will become a reality of darkness.
It can cast out the light of love that God designed
us for with our most beloved connections.
This is the enemy's passion.
This is the enemy's purpose.
BUT
Holy Love persists!
Strong and pure...even in the presence of disappointments.
We are all so weak without Jesus leading us through this world
and through the walk we share with our beloveds.
The enemy knows this.
Jesus gives us the power of love and self-discipline
so that we can rest within the bosom of Holy
Love as it envelops our love connections.
Without Jesus leading us, we are like helpless
sheep as the wolf stalks the flock.
What a revelation!
To understand that love and disappointment
are not mutually exclusive!

You don't think God was disappointed at the River Jordan?
Or at the Jews making their idols?
Or David on the roof?
Or Sampson in his chamber?
It was God's persistent disappointments in His chosen people
that led him to come to us in the flesh.
And it was His Holy Love that led him to the
cross to suffer in unimaginable ways for us
so that we could finally have within us
the shield of His protection and self-discipline and power.
Holy Love is indestructible.

CHAPTER 36

To See Myself Crucified

But he was pierced for our rebellion, crushed for our
sins. He was beaten so we could be whole.
He was whipped so we could be healed.
Isaiah 53:5 (NLT)

God sent Jesus to save humanity. Mary protected and prepared Jesus for His destiny and then released Him as she nailed her own maternal fears and desires and yearnings to the cross. Jesus allowed His preeminence and His royalty to be nailed to the cross along with His flesh. He humbled His stature and magnificence to provide a way for all of humanity to know His love; a Holy Love that is eternal and everlasting. He did this because He is God. God gave Him the strength to do so, even though He suffered momentary separation from His Father. This is all beyond comprehension with my mere mortal mind.

Holy Love...I see it in milliseconds. Like a blood cell traveling through a heart chamber; the moment of a heartbeat. I see it, it's fleeting, and I'm left in awe. Like the beating of a heart, the vision is only momentary. My life in the flesh offers only a foretaste of His Holy Love.

Holy Love is nestled deep within our soul. It's like an ember...a hot coal...a non-extinguishable glow. I know God planted it there, a sacred seed within our DNA.

It's buried deep, tucked securely in the recesses of our heart.

Holy Love: is it the source of that sacred spot on our heart, like the sinoatrial node that initiates the heartbeat of a fetus in the womb?

In the course of our lives, we can magnify that sacred seed and grow it; expanding its warmth and strength and glow. *That* is the fruit of the spirit that uniquely belongs to God.

We have a choice. We can reduce its radiance or we can give it spiritual oxygen that will expand its radiance. I choose oxygen. Life will present moments of hurt and joy...each has the potential to grow the ember into something lovely and nourishing to our soul and to those around us.

My journey, in essence, had become a quest in search of Holy Love. I knew it was there; the source of the ember. These were the original building blocks of my faith in Him. I felt the restless urge to seek Him as I'd gaze at the women chatting quietly behind me in the synagogue in my childhood years. They had no hunger to know who God was. It was His grace that revealed that to me. There simply had to be more to my life than the desolation of my soul that I was living. My spirit was barren.

It was the quickening inside my womb as my daughters reached for me from within that created the quickening of my heart. The heat of my pregnancies illuminated the Holy Love that was growing within me. Still unrecognizable, but unrelenting in its preordained capacity to expand and grow. The heat within my womb offered the possibility of melting that icy wasteland that I lived. For me, the outgrowth from an adulterous life was nothing less than a desolate valley. It was inevitable.

Jesus, in His unrelenting pursuit, used my hurt and my trauma for His own glory. He transformed my shame into love. The only path beyond the wasteland belonged to Jesus.

"Jesus, I pray that you will strengthen me so that I can nail my own maternal pride and desires and yearnings to the cross. Show me how to be my daughters' mother in strength and guidance, as your servant, and not only as their mother in the flesh. Bless my time with my daughters with the light and the glow of your holy Love."

For God, who said, "Let light shine out of the darkness," made his light shine in our hearts to give us the light of the knowledge of God's glory displayed in the face of Christ.
2 Corinthians 4:6 (NIV)

LOVE HARD AS NAILS

"It's in your countenance," you said…. Show me how, I ask.
"You don't own them anymore," you said. "They belong to
me," you said…. Show me how to love that too I ask.
"Make memories," you said…. Show me what's
the best way to do that, I plead.
These were your whisperings. Your guideposts along my
path to remembering how to love like you. And then
the mother of all revelations. You revealed to me that I
needed to use your nails and your cross on my love.
I was in a dark place one afternoon. Wringing my
heart over a conflict with my daughter. I asked you
to lift me out of these dark murky waters. My days of
frequent depression and suffering were long past when I
suddenly found myself in that familiar old swamp.
"Lift me, Jesus! Lift me out!" I prayed.
And instead of you reaching down and me reaching
up to your welcoming grip, you took my arms and
extended them out wide. Freeing, yet vulnerable.
An embrace? Not exactly.
My arms were stretched out wide and I looked up and saw
you hanging there on your cross gazing down at me.
I can still see the light. My arms were engulfed
in light. They were glowing in light.
And you were there before me.

Love hard as nails. Yes! In my mere mortal flesh state, the only
way to love like you is to use your nails upon my body. The only
way to resist the gripping is to nail myself to the cross. You aren't
asking me to literally take nails and do the unthinkable. You are
revealing to me that it would take nails as thick and hard as yours
to maintain my arms out wide in order to stop the grasping.
When you were here with us on this earth in your flesh, you
were able to love and embrace your beloveds. Lazarus, Martha,
Mary, your mother, your apostles. You taught the masses.
You inspired men and women. You ate and you slept.
Like us, your reach was through your voice
and your countenance and through your disciples.
But on the cross!
On the cross, nailed to wood with arms stretched
wide…you could reach all of humanity!
In that seemingly most vulnerable and helpless and
humble state, your power was magnified immeasurably.
Your Holy Spirit could now go to work in earnest.
Like a wind storm pouring through open windows,
or even a breeze finding its way through cracks in the
walls of a house…your Holy Spirit is unstoppable.
It will always find a way in!
I see where you are taking me! I see it! I feel it too!
My outstretched arms…nailed to the cross is
gratefully now an embodied sensation.
It's empowering yet painless.

While the prideful impacts from doing life are unrelenting,
I can now greet them with my arms nailed to the cross.
I can't grasp in this state. I can't attach in this state.
In this state, my countenance will become effortless.
In this state, all moments have memory-making potential.
Love hard as nails is how I can do my work and engage
my community. With every prideful challenge I can
engage this new reality. It becomes a daily practice to
live like this. My responses are softened and graceful.
No angst or grasping. No longstanding suffering.
There is freedom in the Cross.
In this state, the reality that I don't own my
daughters suffers no gnashing of teeth.
In this state, my love for my husband blossoms. I hear his
voice and my heart expands. I see the lines of his face and my
heart expands. I hear his laughter and my heart rejoices.

CHAPTER 37

Musings of Love

I have told you these things so that you will be filled with my joy. Yes, your joy will overflow! This is my commandment: Love each other in the same way I have loved you.
John 15: 11-12 (NLT)

Love is a verb, they say. "It's an action," they say.
I say that love is more than a verb.

All my life, I've longed for it. I wanted to love better. I kept praying, "Teach me to love better."

It was January 2018. Larry and I were putting the Christmas decorations back into the attic. It was gray and bitter cold outside. We had the fireplace going along with Larry's favorite holiday music. It was in a touch…just a light touch on Larry's leg, as he was climbing up into the attic. I lightly touched his jeans, just to reassure him I was there in case he lost his balance. It was my loving action, my verb.

As I touched him, I felt it, and in a millisecond it was life-altering!

It was so fleeting but so very lovely. It was soft like a breath and limitless like air, yet totally encompassing all of me. I knew at that moment and ever more clearly over time, in that fleeting instant, it was God who touched Larry through me. God gave me a foretaste of what Holy Love was. It was Him who lifted my hand to touch my husband's leg!

Love is more than a verb!

The act of touching Larry would have been an act of support so he wouldn't fall; a way to communicate to him I was there. These acts are the face of love, but they are not the soul of love. They are not the source of love. God is the source of love—and I want more of that!

I've always realized and ached for something more from my relationship with my daughters and my family and Larry. I always said I want to feel it, not knowing what *it* was. Who would have thought? A mere moment! With the lightest stroke of a brush on a blank canvas, God would reveal the masterpiece of how He designed us to be or why He designed us at all. Like breadcrumbs on the trail toward His kingdom, piecemeal yet addictive. One "hit," and I'm hooked.

I want to feel it all the time. I want to love better, and I want to love effortlessly and so lovely like that.

Does He make it so fleeting because I couldn't manage its magnitude? Is He protecting me from being swept away by it or with it? He has always said we could not look upon His face, not until He came to earth in His Son. In the same way, I wonder—was that Him who surrounded me in that moment and touched my husband through me? Was it Him?

Up until that moment with Larry, I thought I was learning to love well. But suddenly, I knew how much deeper I could go. Jesus has given me a hint, a glimpse into love's heart.

"Strengthen my capacity for more, Jesus! Make my heart grow more to receive it and give it and manifest it!"

Why did it take sixty-two years for Him to show me? I feel so inadequate sometimes. Why has He been so patient with me? I'm so frustrated by the oh-so-slow pace at which I grow as He reveals these miracles to me.

Love is NOT merely a verb! Love is what drives the actions, and it's so much more!

I want more than the actions, God—there is so little time left! I've wasted so much time in my life caught up in the plastic actions and cerebral efforts and drama that comes out of my own desires and expectations.

In Jesus' name, I pray for God to continue to bless me with more moments like these. Teach me to be love, as He designed.

Loving as a verb is loving with our mere mortal minds. It's not loving with our souls.

Loving as a verb is loving from the outside and extending that love to someone else's outside. That is how I've attempted to do it my whole life.

My life, as with all of us, influenced my development and my manner of loving another human being. My heart broke in my childhood, and I managed as best I could with my heart safely concealed beneath layers of walls to protect its fragile state. Growing up in a home with a foundation of deceit and fraudulence rather than a firm commitment and honor and love left me crippled interpersonally. Family was not cherished. The union of my mother and father was an act. My father tried his best, but my mother wasn't willing or capable of changing her own behavior.

Not until motherhood did I begin to get a clearer sense that something was missing within me. I could barely admit to myself in those self-convicting moments how woefully inadequate my loving was. In my intimate early motherhood moments, I began slowly awakening to the reality of my brokenness and my walls of protection. I didn't understand it at first. I could only glance into it with disdain and self-condemnation and shame. But the walls around my heart began to soften. The alchemy of Him coming closer to me and me allowing it, albeit unknowingly, melted my defenses. Motherhood and the pain of my own disappointment in myself quickened to life the soul of love that He designed for me.

How I wish it didn't take me so long!

Motherhood began to stir in me a longing for the something I still couldn't define. The love I felt for my children as infants and little girls quickened that desire. It gave me a foretaste of the soul of love, a foretaste of who He is. Then love as a verb and the turmoil of life and marriage to their father took hold. In creating the lives of my daughters, my own life was saved. My feeble attempts at loving my babies began to breathe oxygen into my deadened soul.

I sit here today documenting the victory of life over death. Jesus has revealed Himself to me through my own children. Motherhood breaths the soul of love, and with that compassion and mercy becomes effortless. Mothering becomes a reflection of Holy Love. I long to make this my priority over everything I say and do.

> *"Father, help me to be the mother and wife and sister You want me to be. Settle my anxious heart inside of your promise of the Holy love that already is…and has been for all of eternity. Help me, and grow me, and protect my desire and heart from the enemy who would have me focus on the pieces of life that are not of You. Reveal the pathway to me, Jesus! Show me the proper lock for me to put the key into, so I can open the door and release into the ethers the parts of me that keep me from fully loving."*

Holy Love is not a reality that I can dwell within permanently in my mere mortal life. It's as if it's behind the veil in His sacred temple. It's a breath away from us at all times. The ethers prevent me from being thoroughly within it and loving completely within it… because it's who He is…it's what He is.

My seeking Holy Love should be a seeking, rather than assuming that it would be a gaining of it or a becoming it. First, it's too vast, and second it becomes an idol of arrogance.

I am so grateful that my childhood created this hunger within me. In the seeking and in the hunger, I can surrender more and more of myself to Him. I can sacrifice more and more of my grasping to Him, and in the surrendering of myself, His warmth and His love can fill the space left behind. The former nooks and crannies of my pride that I've been able to nail to the cross will yield to His love and His warmth as He takes up more residence within my soul.

"Help me know it more strongly so that when I look upon my loves (Larry, my daughters, my siblings, and the rest of my family), I'll know with all of my heart and mind that Holy Love is coexisting and that in spite of the messy things that pop up and are in the way...that they are only distractions. They are only competitors for my attention and they will wither away like dried fallen leaves. And someday, all the worldly distractions will float away by Your breath upon them.... and all that will be left is Holy love. In your son's name I pray."

The Lord your God will drive those nations out ahead of you little by little. You will not clear them away all at once, otherwise the wild animals would multiply too quickly for you. But the Lord your God will hand them over to you.
Deuteronomy 7:22-23 (NLT)

Those who have been ransomed by the Lord will return.
They will enter Jerusalem singing,
Crowned with everlasting joy.
Sorrow and mourning will disappear,
And they will be filled with joy and gladness.
Isaiah 51:11(NLT)

THE POWER OF HIS LOVE

When does human love merge and transform into Holy Love?
In the messy blunders and waning of a mere mortal
love; with our meager capacity to see through it
all...the realm of Holy Love sits in waiting.
Holy Love is within reach...just beyond "the curtain."
The veil conceals it from us. The veil is the back side of
the tapestry; the fabric of our earthly relationships.
The underbelly of our lives.
I want so urgently to remove the veil...but I think You won't
allow that until You allow it. It's Your timing, not mine.
Maybe it's not possible until You return.
But You occasionally give me a glimpse!
It's amazing!
Spectacular and overwhelming.
Sweet overwhelm...it's breathtaking!
It's too big for my mere mortal eyes.
In the meantime, You pull back the curtain
momentarily to reveal eternity to me.
Holy Love is Your eternity.
Like my sweet nephew, at two years old, said as he
pointed to the full moon over the ocean: "I want it!"
"Not yet, my sweet...not yet..."
In faith, in hope. You reveal Holy Love to me as Your promise.

CHAPTER 38

The Garden of My Life

The Lord will comfort Israel again and have pity
on her ruins. Her desert will blossom like Eden, her
barren wilderness like a garden of the Lord.
Joy and gladness will be found there. Songs
of thanksgiving will fill the air.
Isaiah 51:3 (NLT)

I became a gardening lover as I approached the latter third of my life. As a young teenager the seed for the love of gardening was planted. I spent sweet moments with my father as he landscaped our property in our new home in Baltimore County. He eventually handed the project over to me, as I dabbled in flowers and edibles. Several decades later I find myself finding both joy and peace as I cultivate beauty in my own suburban front yard garden.

My front yard has God's signature all over it. If not for Him, I would not be free today nor would there be a garden in my life. My garden is a manifestation of my journey thus far. Gardening has taught me patience as well as letting go. The weather and seasonal changes require me to practice the adage 'let go and let God'.

I never fail to marvel at the view from my front porch. I look out at the lush growth. It's a manicured jungle, intentional chaos. It's so much like life; simultaneously messy and stunning.

We make choices at various crossroads that influence our earthly journey forever. For example, had I known ten years ago that I would develop a passion for edible gardens, I would have never planted the river birch in my front yard. Its tall elegance matches its shade, limiting my gardening possibilities in an already shady front yard.

I work with what I have left. The only consistent sunny patch of lawn in my front yard is a five-by-thirty-foot strip along my driveway. The summer of 2016 was an explosion of life magnificent to behold. My front yard was an intentional, chaotic array of clover and mint amongst five varieties of squash, tomatoes, cucumbers, and string beans. Marigolds, strategically planted, coordinate their efforts with aromatic mint to keep pests and deer down to a minimum. Specific edible weeds flourish among my tomatoes and beans. Oh, the wild magnificence when you let nature have its way with your garden!

It's a reflection of my life as a latecomer to Christ. There are so many decisions I'd not have made, or actions I wish I had done differently. Here I am at sixty-two, manifesting my vitality within the boundaries of my own limitations.

My life is imperfect. It's a blend of mended relationships that burst forth with love like the striking strips of red or deep yellow in my garden. While, because of the shady conditions, there is not as much color in my garden as I'd like, it is exquisite nonetheless. While there are not as many loving and sweet memories as I'd like, my life is now magnificent to behold. I think about what it must be like for the first meal to a starving person; the tastes explode with such intensity that the flavor lingers in one's memory indelibly. Or the joy of a color-blind person who with today's technology can suddenly see color. For such a person, life goes from black and white to permanent technicolor! For me, each conflict-free, drama-free, and peaceful moment leaves me in awe. The capacity to savor healed and loving relationships is magnified tenfold.

There is stunning satisfaction and sweet reverie that comes with a mended and healed life. The juxtaposition of the sorrow and the suffering with the explosion of sweetness and abundance leaves me in knee-dropping gratitude to my Savior, Jesus Christ.

The imperfection of my garden thrills me. Who would think

that there is beauty and satisfaction in imperfection? Our strivings for perfection are probably by His design because it develops our desire for the divine. The miracle of beauty in imperfection is how I suspect He sees us.

He loves us so much that He gifts us with His grace and mercy as we make our way on our life journey toward His kingdom.

The Lord will guide you continually, giving you
water when you are dry and restoring your strength.
You will be like a well-watered garden,

like an ever-flowing spring. Some of you will rebuild the deserted
ruins of your cities. Then you will be known as a rebuilder of walls
and a restorer of homes.
Isaiah 58:11-12 (NLT)

———————— ✦✦◆✦✦ ————————

One of my favorite times of the year is mid-May through the end of October. It's become my sweet spot of my life to sit and gaze out onto my front yard. It's the space between the inhale and the exhale of the onset of spring and end of autumn when the work I've created in my front garden manifests the partnership between me and Jesus.

Every time I sit on my front porch and gaze out at it I see His work and I'm in awe. I remember the desert, like scorched earth, that was once my life. I recall the sterile ground and thorny patches of growing up in an adulterous home and enduring my own loveless first marriage. In milliseconds I can recall decades of estrangement between my soulmate sister and myself. I recall my self-righteous lens through which I viewed people. I revisit the judgmental and unloving posture with the people that mattered most in my life. The measuring stick with which I'd view myself was based in school grades or credentials or earned of hard work. The tasks and goals completed each day defined my worthiness or lovability. These cerebralized interpretations of my life and life in general began a slow and gradual dismantling as God's perspective and His view of me and my life took hold.

My front yard is now *love* in shades of green. There are sunny patches where I've planted plants that can flower and bear fruit. There are patches of wild edibles like dandelions and chickweed that I selectively allow to flourish because of their nutritional value. I've learned the value of weeds, just as I've learned the value of a painful journey whose lessons have, by the grace of God, not been wasted on me. My yard boasts enchantment in organized chaos. It's so charming that it attracts the children on my street who clamor to help me garden and water the plants. From the blueberry bushes that have not yet flourished but are learning to grow, to the volunteer thorny wild raspberry briar patches that I've granted residence, the yard is like a testament to my journey thus far.

It has too much shade because of a tree I planted ten years ago, a decision made prior to my coming of age as an edible gardener. So, I work with what I have and God's miracle of nature does the rest. I tweak and He breathes life. He determines the shades and depths of color and magnitude of abundance, and I design the patterning of plants and color. I provide the compost and thoughtful placement of it, and He provides the miracle of soil that has nourishment.

It's an organized chaos, and it is magnificent. One neighbor says she smells a sweet fragrance every time she walks by it long beyond the April bloom of the lilac bush I planted for Larry years ago. The children love to pick and smell the chocolate mint, and the bumblebees make a home in my shed because they feast on the flowering catnip and catmint beside my sidewalk. From the daffodils that proliferate throughout my yard in April and May, or the relentless volunteer black-eyed Susans that feed the goldfinches in August and September, to the volunteer cucumbers and squash alongside my heirloom tomato plants and string beans, my yard bursts the seams of nature's heart. It soothes in its enchantment and delights in its vitality. It brings me a joy that I can only feebly attempt to put into words here. I gaze upon it and am simultaneously seeing the former desert of my life and the promised land on the other side of the parted sea.

◆◆◆◆◆

My yard manifests the glory of my life as compared to the suffering of my past. I know that it is only a foreshadow of the glory of the things to come. God has not even created words for me to describe that. I rest in contentment at that inability. There is comfort in the not knowing it in detail because beyond Revelations, He has promised wonders beyond my understanding or imagination.

"It is like a tiny mustard seed that a man planted in
a garden; it grows and becomes like a tree,
and the birds make nests in its branches."
Luke 13:19 (NLT)

I gaze out on my garden in mid-September. Autumn is easing into our direction. I feel it in the air as a crisp puff of breeze brushes my cheek. I love watching the morning sunlight that casts upon the ground. It makes its way, reliably but slowly, onto my waiting garden. The spent growth that remains is getting tired, yet is earnest for the sunlight; like a lover with outstretched arms craving more time with his beloved.

The tomato plants are becoming spindly with feeble attempts at new fruit. The mint is lanky and overgrown. I watch goldfinches nibbling on what's left of the black-eyed Susan seed pods that still stand tall on their fading stalks. Mildewy squash leaves and marigolds command the spaces now. Hydrangeas are morphing toward their burgundy hue. My urge to tweak and weed is diminishing. Yet, there is a settled contentment in realizing the finished product of this particular season. It's a mirror of my life's journey with Jesus watching over me as I return to my reflections on my daughters and my motherhood journey with them.

Without Jesus within me, I'd have come to this bend in the road of motherhood, white-knuckled from my own feeble efforts to do it well. With the Holy Spirit guiding my heart and mind and behavior, I can finally say that I've given what I can give. I've learned what it is to love with an open heart.

If I had gone it alone, my daughters would have received merely the contrived and intentional efforts from a mother who was thinking her way to doing her best by them. I would have been making the healthiest meals, following the culture's *best parenting* guidelines, trying to control my temper and hide my dissatisfactions. I'd have metaphorically been driving my daughters down the highway of our life together with that tight grip on the steering wheel.

With Christ, my relationship with my daughters now has the sweet kiss of His blessing. My interactions and conversations are manifestations of an open-armed love that could only come from my surrender. No more grasping, no more gripping, and no more angst or white knuckles. This is not to suggest that it's always a smooth and easy ride. There are still bumps in the road. Those occasional interactions when I must rein in my attempts to impose my will upon my children are thankfully coming with less frequency. The overriding experience is now one of grace and acceptance together. And the joy that Jesus offers us surrounds and permeates it all.

There is now an ease and enough opening to allow the sweet intermingling of separate souls. It's a maternal love at its best, interwoven with moments of Holy Love. These moments are the foreshadowing of what is to come in His kingdom.

I can rest in the comfort of knowing that when my time comes…I will have finally given all I had to give; that I will have done my best, and I had run a good race. There is peace in that.

> *The Sovereign Lord will show his justice to the nations*
> *of the world. Everyone will praise him!*
> *His righteousness will be like a garden in early*
> *spring, with plants springing up everywhere.*
> **Isaiah 61:11 (NLT)**

I HEAR YOUR BREATH

You whispered it.
Your breath barely perceptible…yet a hurricane.
Raindrops upon my roof…yet a tsunami.
You sacrificed everything for me!
You gave up everything for me!
You relinquished your glory, your power…everything!
I ask you to show me; teach me; shape me to love like you!
Teach me Holy Love.
And today you whispered back,
"Put down your mantel. Lay it down and let it go.
Release your grasp on the things of the world.
The passion, the youth, the fantasies, the
expectations, the strivings.
You are holding onto the things of the past. Let them go.
Let them go like I let go of everything for your sake.
When you nail them to the cross, then you
allow Me to become your passion fully.
When I become your passion, then will you love
your beloveds with passion and holiness.
In order to receive, you must release.
When you release your grip on these things in your world, then
I can fully dwell within; only then will I become your passion
fully…and then the fire of Holy Love will begin to manifest. By
loving Me fully, you can love your husband fully; your children
fully; your friends and family and work fully…all of it!"

CHAPTER 39

A Tribute to Love and Marriage

I have entered my garden, my treasure, my bride!
I gather myrrh with my spices and eat honeycomb with
my honey. I drink wine with my milk. Oh, lover and
beloved, eat and drink! Yes, drink deeply of your love!
Song of Songs 5:1 (NLT)

In October 2017, my oldest daughter got married. It was one of the happiest days of my life, because my immediate family was there along with Larry and me. As I gazed across our banquet table and saw my extended family all celebrating with the same joy and love for my daughter I was aware that we had crossed 'that river Jordan'. We had been through so much pain and angst, yet the love and the healing played victor.

What follows is a letter I read to my daughter and new son-in-law at their wedding reception.

When you were about three years old you asked me, "Mom…can we get married someday?"

I remember the moment. I had been out for a few hours and you were with Ruth the babysitter. You were at the playground and you spotted me coming up the sidewalk to get you. You came running down the sidewalk and flung yourself into my arms. I remember it as clearly as you are sitting here right now. I don't even know how at such a young age you knew what "married" even meant. You must have picked it up on a Disney movie or something. I don't recall what I said exactly in response, but I remember the holding...the hugs and the kisses. I think I must have said something like, "I love you bigger than the sky and I always will...and that's even better."

My children are my heart. You will understand that better once you become a mother.

To my new son, I want you to know, that with my blessing, I relinquish that marriage vow to you. I know how much you love your wife and I know you will protect her in all ways. And that means more to me than you could know.

In many ways, I've concluded that my life has been about discovering what love really is.

It's a mysterious thing. We try to capture it in a ring...a dress...a celebration. But it's so much more than that.

My blessing for you both is that you grow to discover how deep and timeless your love will become through the years. This celebration really marks the beginning of that journey for the two of you.

Love is not something you can touch. It's something that your heart reveals to you in between beats. You'll feel it in the whispers between the inhale and the exhale. The love I am talking about is formless. It's timeless...and it's the sweetest gift you've yet to discover.

They say that love is a verb...an action. It's forgiveness, and patience and kindness, and slow to anger, and persevering and trusting, to name a few. What I'm talking about, though, is the something that is the foundation of all of these actions. When you discover it in those sweetest of moments, know that it's real... in fact, it's more real than this moment in front of you right now.

The sweetest of all gifts that marriage will provide for you is that you will discover what it means to cherish one another. To cherish the gift that you've been given in each other is actually the greatest gift of all. It's the prize. That's what the journey is for.

Life will hit you with so many challenges...good and bad...joyful and sad. There will be both celebrations and sorrows. As you walk those paths...you are going to do it together. And in that doing...in those actions... you build your capacity to discover the heart beneath it all. That's where you will discover the cherishing.

Recently someone said to me that life is like a tapestry and that we tend to experience our lives from the back side of the tapestry. The knots and muted tones and tangled patterns... It's colorful but also messy. But turn the tapestry around to the front side...and it is magnificent to behold. It's brilliant. It will take your breath away. And that's the cherishing.

Larry has taught me the phrase "sadness shared is halved, and joy shared is doubled." I say, that is what makes the fabric of the tapestry we call a marriage. That's also where the cherishing can reveal itself to you.

The funny thing about life and marriage is that we have a tendency to focus on the back side of that tapestry. It's human nature. And we forget that we are only looking at the underbelly of our lives.

My prayers for you both are that you will have many moments when you will capture glimpses of the front side of your own unique tapestry. And that over time you'll develop the ability to linger there for longer and longer periods of time. And that you will come to discover the cherishing of each other and your life together.

In the meantime… Love on each other a lot…support each other, share your joys and your sorrows. Grow together. Have health and prosper in all ways. Perfect the tapestry you are beginning to design that will be uniquely yours.

I love you both unconditionally always and in all ways.

Love

Mom

> *This is my command: Love each other.*
> **John 15:17 (NLT)**

PAVING STONES

Romantic love.
parental love.
platonic love....
They pave the way to Holy Love.
And simultaneously, Holy love is the force
that creates these paving stones.
We know that it is God who created love...who IS love.
We must crawl before we can walk.
And we must walk before we can run.
Or fly!
Our experience of platonic and familial and
parental love are all sourced to us by Him.
He is giving us the building blocks to
become stronger in how we love.
Jesus is gifting us the opportunity to practice
real love...His love...Holy Love.
God's royal heart is the cornerstone of Holy Love.

CHAPTER 40

The Best Inheritance

Dear friends, since God loved us that much,
We surely ought to love each other. No one has ever seen
God. But if we love each other, God lives in us,
and his love is brought to full expression in us.
1 John 4: 11-12 (NLT)

Dear as I held you close in my arms
Angels were singing a hymn to your charms
Two hearts gently beating murmuring low
Darling I love you so

Could we but recall
That sweet moment sublime
We'd find that our love
Is unaltered by time

("Anniversary Song," Al Jolson)

There is a scene in the movie *The Al Jolson Story* where Al Jolson is watching his parents dancing as he sings their favorite song, "Anniversary Song." This was their fiftieth anniversary and Al's father asked him to sing for them while they danced. I was deeply touched by the look the son gave his parents as he sang for them. The love his mother and father shared, expressed as they gazed into each other's eyes, and the love Al Jolson expressed in his gazing at them as he sang, was exquisite. Was it his love for them, or was it his expression of awe over the love his parents shared for each other that struck me? It was this scene, in the movie, when I came to understand the power of cherishing our loved ones.

To cherish our beloveds is how the Lord has designed His Holy Love to manifest in our relationships as we walk this worldly journey. The greatest gift parents can pass down to their children is to cherish each other. This is greater than any financial inheritance that you could pass down.

A child gazes upon her parents and their loving dance with each other, and what gets imprinted is the eternal seal of Holy Love. The love between two parents fills the ethers within a familial home and permeates the soul of each child within those walls.

Cherishing becomes the fragrance that perfumes throughout the home. It is the most nourishing source of sustenance that can carry a child into adulthood. It can lay the foundation for a legacy of Holy Love to manifest within a home and beyond; and it is a blueprint of how to allow Holy Love to show up in the flesh. Holy Love is at the core of all our love connections. It exists as pure potential for our most treasured relationships. It is the source of what can manifest into cherishing another person.

What a blessing for a child, to receive this legacy! It lays the groundwork that can promise the possibility to repeat itself in their own life and marriage. This I believe is by God's design.

We fall in love and meld our love experience with passion. The heat of passion can lay the foundation for a lasting relationship. As life *gets in the way* in the creation of a family, work, house, and domestic realities, the *in love* can morph into an assumption of love and solidarity. As Tevya's wife in *Fiddler on the Roof* asks her husband, "Do you love me?" Tevya responds with questioning her doubt since he has lived all the years with her with children and poverty and political unrest and more in Russia. The permutations of marriage and family can make us *forget* our *in love* days when what we really are doing is becoming distracted from our hearts. We overlook the blessings. We miss the moments where Holy Love reveals itself. Its like clouds, that part for a brief moment, revealing a brilliant clear blue sky. Here one moment and then gone.

Cherishing is what showed up as woefully missing in my life until I married and learned how to love well in my second marriage. Loving well did not come naturally to me, and it is an ongoing *learning* process even today. In the absence of my parents' ability to manifest a healthy cherishing love in my home, it left me with the task of developing that ability on my own. Jesus in his relentless work within me changed my heart so I could learn how to love. He used my receptivity to His craftsmanship.

Cherishing a spouse or a child places a value onto that person that has nothing to do with our own ego or pride. It is not about expectations, or agendas or judgments, and it holds firm even in the presence of disappointments. It is not a clinging possessiveness, nor is it entitlement or codependence.

Cherishing is an unconditional state of the heart that extends Holy Love into our real-life relationships. It is kind and adoring. Cherishing is patient, and it attempts to rise up our loved ones. It seeks to listen and be present. It is the fruit of the spirit as God designed. Its intention is to uphold the treasure that is our beloveds. Yes, a treasure!

The potential to cherish our beloveds is the possibility for all of us. Crossing the threshold into my *rebirth* in Christ has been nothing less than miraculous. Jesus took this broken heart of mine and allowed it to reopen to allow for the love of my most treasured relationships to finally begin to blossom. Glimpses into His Holy Love was life-altering because it sealed my hope in the promises He has made for our eternal journey. And in that realization, I could come to celebrate these precious relationships.

With God, all we need are glimpses. Milli-moments of His light or word or whisper are life-altering because He is eternal. He is omnipotent. He is sovereign. The lord of the universe is Holy Love, and that is His legacy. He offers it to us as our inheritance.

Lord, you alone are my inheritance, my cup of blessing.
You guard all that is mine. The land you have given me
is a pleasant land. What a wonderful inheritance!
Psalm 16:5-6 (NLT)

THE PRACTICED EYE

To see beyond the flesh
Beyond the sin
Beyond the emotional blemishes that this
journey here on earth creates.
To be able to peer beyond the veil of another
and into the heart of who they are…
…who God designed them to be.
To become a master at seeing beyond the veil of
humanity so I can see the shimmering gems that are
scattered throughout the pasture of my life.
Yes! They are there!
The gems!
The uncut diamonds!
The precious stars!
They are His creation, and I will myself to practice every day, the
art of seeing these scattered masterpieces that surround my life!

CHAPTER 41

Love as Sacrifice

For God has not given us a spirit of fear and timidity,
but of power, love and self-discipline.
2 Timothy 1: 7 (NLT)

As Jesus has escorted me through this discovery of Holy Love, he revealed to me that it is through relinquishing my pride that I can love more fully. I can begin to approach the realm of loving that He is guiding all of us toward.

It's a practice and a discipline; the putting down my pride; the surrendering my attachment to my own sense of myself. It's like developing the psychic muscle to master the art of release. It's in obedience to Jesus that I relax my grip on whatever I'm attached to in a potential loving moment.

Whether it's an expectation, a disappointment, or a judgment, the possibilities are endless when my pride is in control. When I release my grip on these things I can choose to settle into gratitude. It's not that I can't set limits when appropriate, or admonish when called for. Releasing my grip on my own pride is also not about me becoming a doormat or not being assertive.

When an interaction is with a loved one whom I cherish, then discerning when my pride is in the way allows me to make choices for the sake of the relationship. This can become my guiding principle. This is when I can choose to sacrifice my own pride and allow gratitude to guide me. It's in gratitude that I can rediscover the loving connections that I crave. Gratitude is a discipline that can only be practiced with a will to surrender. We continually must sacrifice what we hold dear in the flesh, in our worldly attachments, in our pride and in our sin. The Lord commands continually throughout the Bible that we leave our idols behind. He commands the Jews to burn and destroy the idols because they are not of Him. Idols are also the fabrications of our own worldviews.

> *Do not make idols or set up carved images, or sacred pillars,*
> *or sculptured stones in your land so you may worship them.*
> *I am the Lord your God.* **Leviticus 26:1 (NLT)**

Love, like gratitude, is also a sacrifice. It is always an act of faith. I say this because in order to fully love, we must die to ourselves; and only the love and strength of the Holy Spirit can strengthen our capacity to do this.

Even gratitude for *good times* is a sacrifice because, when we appreciate what God has done in our lives, we don't attach ownership to these good times. We release even those to the Lord.

God has given us the capacity for self-discipline and this is an offspring of our will. Self-discipline is a fruit of the spirit as God designed us. Its purpose is to develop our capacity for surrender and thus for gratitude. All of this is in the service of Holy Love.

I share my story, hoping you can find some freedom as well. Maybe my sorrow and searching of my own path will strike a chord with yours. As I reveal my own secrets, I invite you to allow it to shed light into your own. Light always casts out the darkness.

My story is for all Christians and seekers. I especially write it for my Jewish people. To my Jewish brothers and sisters: I call to you with love and urgency to allow your hearts to see these words and feel their familiarity. Our Old Testament is the foundational foreshadow of His purpose and promise to us as His first chosen.

Jesus was born out of the loins of our ancestors, and I hope to entice you to look beyond the veil of what we've been taught who Jesus is.

I have done my best to do Him justice with pen in hand. It's in obedience that I have set pen to paper.

God has revealed to me that Holy Love is all there is.

The rest is story.

SWEET OVERWHELM

Why, when I sit with You and feel You surrounding me…
and feel your breath upon me,
do I shed these tears?
I don't feel sadness in these moments.
It's not grief or joy…it's something more;
and I have no word for it.
But I can tell you this…
It's a flood of sweet overwhelm and the surrender
into awareness of you and your love.
Like waves merging into each other on the ocean's edge.
Maybe the tears are a continual cleansing of
deep sorrow, mixed with grief and regret.
They are the years of a life when I resisted your call.
Let them come…
Let them roll continuously on from the ocean of my soul.
Cleanse me, Jesus!
Heal me, Jesus!

SWEET OVERWHELM
EPILOGUE

Then Christ will make his home in your hearts as you trust in him. Your roots will grow down into God's love and keep you strong. And may you have the power to understand, as all God's people should, how wide, how long, how high, and how deep his love is. May you experience the love of Christ, though it is too great to understand fully. Then you will be made complete with all the fullness of life and power that comes from God.
Ephesians 3: 17-18 (NLT)

As I sit on my front porch taking in the visual sweetness of my gardens, I once again begin reflecting on how far I've traveled in my sixty-five years. I marvel at the juxtaposition of the imperfections in both my garden and my life thus far, along with the sweet beauty of a job well done. My partnership with Jesus has brought forth abundance and manifested His grace and mercy in multiple shades of green.

I marvel at the miracle of sweet bonds that have remained intact throughout the briar patch earth path of my journey until the fifth decade of my life.

In gratitude I turn my gaze to my own siblings. It would be believable if I had told people that my sister and my brother and I had only occasional contact and that email had become our convenient source of rare communications. After all, how can any relationship flourish from a scorched stump in a dried-up valley?

But this has not been the case. I revel at the bond and love that

247

my siblings and I share. We speak as often as possible. We share holidays when we can, and we also take advantage of the texting and social media platforms that keep us connected. This is possible because the love of our sibling bond kept its strength. I know that this has been by the grace of God, who has gifted us with a bond that is inseverable. I can see it and feel it with its breath of fragrance, and it overwhelms me with gratitude.

When my nephew died, my brother was by my sister's side within hours as he and his family dropped their own matters in New Jersey and drove straight home to Maryland. When my sister-in-law had bilateral knee surgery, I spent her first full weekend home with her in New Jersey to tend to her. I retained vigil during the first twelve months of my sister's grief over losing her son. No matter where or who I was with, if my sister called me, I'd answer. I couldn't remove her pain or turn back time for her; but I could hold the space for her suffering. When my niece got married, my brother and our cousin and I managed the care of my wheelchair-bound mother at the reception so my sister and niece could celebrate without worries or unpleasantness. These are only a few examples of our doing love with each other and for each other. Our *love as verbs*. In essence, my siblings and I have been undeterred in the solidarity and loving loyalty we have toward each other.

The relationships between my daughters and me are now healed and growing beautifully. As I "mother" my daughters, who are young adults, the Holy Spirit guides me in how to bring forward my best self on their behalf. Jesus guides me through my marriage to Larry, who has emerged as my best friend in addition to being my spouse and my lover.

It's the doing of motherhood and marriage in partnership with Jesus that has brought peace and flourishing into this previously barren valley that was my spirit. God has blessed me with a joy that has His signature all over it, and He has commanded me to cease from stealing it away from myself. It's with this conviction and His command that I can take ownership of that joy as I sojourn on with all of my loved ones. In Jesus' continued shepherding of me I have developed intolerance to angst or conflict with my family. Jesus continues to help me see and to help me be in love with every one of them. I no longer linger in the shadow of relationship conflicts.

But the Holy Spirit produces this kind of fruit in our lives:
JOY, peace, patience, kindness, goodness, faithfulness.
Galatians 5:22 (NLT)

For me, practicing arms extended and nailed to the cross, I grow in my ability to love all of my family in holiness. Healing of my own heart and family wounds creates a foundation to allow me to learn how to spread this joy to the world around me.

I am overwhelmed with joy in the Lord my God! For he
has dressed me with the clothing of salvation and draped
me in a robe of righteousness. I am like a bridegroom
dressed for his wedding or a bride with her jewels.
Isaiah 61:10 (NLT)

In sweet overwhelm I marvel at the results of God's healing hand.
As my sister said to me so many years before, *"Jill, you've seen the light. You'll never go back into the darkness."*
Jesus has stepped into the darkness that consumed my spirit, and now there is light where once darkness dwelled.
Hallelujah!

For God who said, "Let there be light in the darkness," has
made this light shine in our hearts so we could know the glory
of God that is seen in the face of Jesus Christ. We now have
this light shining in our hearts, but we ourselves are like fragile
clay jars containing this great treasure. This makes it clear
that our great power is from God, not from ourselves.
2 Corinthians 4: 6-7 (NLT)

HOLY LOVE PRAYER

Father, in Your Son's name, I pray for Your blessing over my heart.
I pray for Your healing and Your miraculous grace and mercy.
Make my heart big.
Make it lovely.
Make it loving.
Make it holy.
Make it dominate my waking and my sleeping.
Make this my passion.
Make this my mission.
Make this my priority over everything I say and do.

If you enjoyed this book, will you consider
sharing the message to others?

- Mention the book in a Facebook or Instagram or Pinterest post.
- Recommend this book to those in your small group, book club, workplace, and classes.
- Head over to FACEBOOK: Holy Love: a Memoir of Sorrow to Glory. "LIKE" the page, and post a comment as to what you enjoyed the most.
- INSTAGRAM: AUTHOR-J.E.SMITH
- Pick up a copy for someone you know who would be inspired and encouraged by the message of this book.
- Write a book review online.